THE TRAGEDY OF
KING
LEWIS
THE SIXTEENTH

THE TRAGEDY OF
KING
LEWIS
THE SIXTEENTH

a modern dramatization

DAVID LANE

TATE PUBLISHING
AND ENTERPRISES, LLC

Published by Tate Publishing & Enterprises, LLC
127 E. Trade Center Terrace | Mustang, Oklahoma 73064 USA
1.888.361.9473 | www.tatepublishing.com

Tate Publishing is committed to excellence in the publishing industry. The company reflects the philosophy established by the founders, based on Psalm 68:11,
"The Lord gave the word and great was the company of those who published it."

Published in the United States of America

ISBN: 978-1-61346-282-9
1. Performing Arts, Theater, Stagecraft
2. Performing Arts, Theater, General
12.04.10

DEDICATION

In memory of my father and my mother.

Requiescant in pace.

PREFACE

In the play that gives its title to this volume, the reader will notice that the names of the characters have been anglicized. I have done so because the work is is a piece of poetry in English and according to once-traditional practice should generally be as English as practicable. (Such was the use of Shakespeare.)

Throughout this volume, I have used regular traditional metrics and the traditional language of poetry universal from the time of Homer to the poets immediately preceding the First World War, at which time persons such as Ezra Pound and T. S. Eliot, influenced by Idealist aesthetics and no doubt by Wordsworth (and, I should say, by the utilitarian tenor prevalent in the West), had the temerity to jettison from their craft archaic and poetic diction and regular metrics. It is a sad fact that the works of poets at present are often awkward, sometimes vulgar, prose impoverished in diction.

Believing that the timelessness of the Classic style might be revived to advantage, I had in mind Gilbert Murray's evocative words on the Classic tradition in poetry: "The magic of Memory [is] at work . . . the 'waker of longing,' the enchantress who turns the common to the heavenly and fills men's eyes with tears because the things that are now past were so beautiful." Because this tradition is largely forgotten, I suggest to those who prize the new that this play represents a new direction in poetry and drama.

Accordingly, "The Tragedy of King Lewis the Sixteenth" is written entirely in blank verse. In composing it, I set out to make ample use of the inexhaustible riches of the English language, especially those veins yet extant that for a century have lain unmined. I wished also to write a play (a social and highly public genre) studying the character of a relatively modern historical figure presented somewhat in the mould of the ancient Greek and Elizabethan stages. The figure I chose, Louis XVI of France, and the revolutionary times in which he lived and died are still highly germane to the present day, in both the dimension of human nature and the still unsettled, not to say vexed, question of modernity, especially since the Enlightenment.

DRAMATIS PERSONAE

King Lewis XVI

Queen Mary Antoinette, wife to the King

Madame Elizabeth, sister to the King

Charles, Count of Artois, younger brother to the King

Lewis Charles, the Dauphin

Mary Theresa Charlotte (Madame Royale), the Dauphine

St. Margaret Mary Alacoque

St. Lewis IX

A Demon

James Necker, Director of the Treasury

Count de Montmorin, minister to the King

Count de la Luzerne, minister to the King

First Parliamentarian

Second Parliamentarian

Cardinal de la Rochefoucauld

Mgr. Le Clerc de Juigné, Archbishop of Paris

A Chamberlain

Lewis Philip, Duke of Orleans, cousin to the King

Countess de Coigny, friend to the Duke of Orleans

An Aged Guest

M. Adrian Duport, friend to the Duke of Orleans

John Paul Marat, radical journalist and revolutionary

A Sentry

A Gentleman of the King's hunting party
Baron de Besenval, lieutenant colonel in the Royal Army
Count de Saint-Priest, counselor to the King
Marquis de la Tour Du Pin, counselor to the King
Prince de Beauveau, counselor to the King
The Mob
Marquis de Lafayette,
      Commander-in-Chief of the National Guard
A Coachman
Count von Fersen, friend to the Royal Family
Drouet, a postmaster
Romeuf, Aide-de-Camp to the Marquis de Lafayette
George James Danton, member of the Paris Commune
Peter Lewis Roederer, Syndic of the Department of Paris
John Francis Honoré Merlet, President of the Legislative Assembly
Francis Chabot, deputy of the Legislative Assembly
A Deputy of the Legislative Assembly
Captain Durler, Commander of the Swiss Guards
Four rioters
William Christian de Malesherbes, defense counsel to the King
Raymond Romain, Count de Sèze, defense counsel to the King
Bertrand Barère, President of the Convention
Cléry, valet de chambre to the King

Dominic Joseph Garat, deputy of the Convention
Philip Antony Grouvelle, deputy of the Convention
Abbé Edgeworth de Firmont, confessor to the King
Commander of the Guard at the guillotine

ACT 1

Scene 1

[*St. Margaret Mary Alacoque clothed in a nun's habit stands in the moonlit sky above Paris, the rooftops of which are visible below. She faces at some distance a bank of clouds whence presently St. Lewis IX emerges in armour and crowned.*]

St. Margaret Mary Alacoque

O thou that look'st a sire and saint of France,
  Who fleet'st like thought—nay, heart-driv'n prayer—
from forth
  Yond airy drift pearled o'er of the minist'ring moon,
  Didst thou, as I, descend this fatal night
  To mourn th' impending death and seasonable
  Of France, whose slated tow'rs beneath our strides
  Yet sleep?

St. Lewis IX

        Thy eyes, good saint, which owe to high
Ordaining sight of our supernal Good
Can hardly fail at ginning kings from clouds.
I walk and weep the night, I yield thee; more,
Of God I beg a cendiary grace
That like the catapulted brand aleap
The battlement may find the keep of France,
E'vn Lewis, Our latter son now reigning sev'nth

So named from Us. I would this fire of grace
His sometime chill—his something stolid—heart
Might warm and stir, might temper sure and poise
His something flaccid—sometime wobbling—mind;
For more by much than all th' anointed heads
That bare the glittering weight of France shall this
King know it for a brist'ling round of thorns.

    If sipping in this cordial of grace—
His warmth and coolth, his fleece of lenity
And plate of rigour, he shall right array
Ere he should find Him naked to the knots
And plummets of the wielded scorpion—
This inward, yea his outward, bodiment,
Indeed the frame and quick of France, may not
Be felled all flat and altogether killed.

St. Margaret Mary Alacoque

Oh, grant him God this viewless fire of grace!
The iron tongue of years is twitched ev'n now
To toll full throat the fatal hundredyear
Of leav'ning impudence. Oh softly! nose
You not malarias—as they were ris'n
From wards and walks sunk deeply netherwards
Of any mews that reek below o' nights?

[*Suddenly and amidst an eruption of fire and smoke,
a frightful demon enters from below and rushes with men-
ace to the two saints, who remain quite calm. (It is desirable
that in the execution of this entrance the audience be rendered
breathless.)*]

The Demon

O Hell! Hell! Hell! Paris will
Be Hell! The Heart we legions hate was scorned
Below these hundred years agone, and France
Has slowly rotted—hearts and minds—till it
Must drop betimes within the patient yawn
Of our long-slav'ring jaws. For such a guest
What tortures sweet, what terrors exquisite
Could we in grateful turn have failed to lade
With liberal hand (or claw?) the groaning board?

St. Margaret Mary Alacoque

As forward he as ignorance unblushed.

The Demon

The fourteenth Lud—and, since, the royal whelps,
Whose inward eyes were ever lidded fast,
Those elder twain by simple woman's flesh,
That younger by the simple failure in
The royal fisc—these three, I say, have brought
To happy nil that fell request—the pledge
Of France to Him on high—which ev'n that Heart
Of our discomfit badest thee, dame saint,
To bring to France's very person for
A ready, ratheripe consummation. Ha!
O salted silken tailcoats, fainéants
To Hell's prone Mayor! O torpid and obtuse,
These faithless, *useful,* kings and dolphins, toads
Of Hell—say rather frogs of Phlegethon!

St. Lewis IX

O have a reck and comely more thy croak
Of words lest soon I ring from out this thigh
This living sword, thou bloated rennet-bag
Of curdling sin, and sink it deep within
Thy meatless, unarticulated limbs,
Who clott'st all suck of mercy in the breast.

The Demon

Relent, Most Christian Majesty!—But are
They not an addle crown, of wingèd zeal
Found void? Be quite as may, my cordial foes,
For whom I have an everlasting rod
In pickle, our earthly minions yonder stick
At naught, who haply rave ev'n now beneath
Fierce mares of envy ris'n from Hell to stride
Their lab'ring lungs. 'Tis true, I own, their breasts
Of godly milk be clotted. Monstrous biggs
They grow with vitriol astrut, wherewith
That ancient fabric raised of Clovis rude
And odiously lavered to dissolve,
That then rough boars may tear and grind in lambs.

St. Margaret Mary Alacoque

O Heart of Christ still scorned, Who tend'rest still
Thy wayward ones who headlong rush to spend
The long forever supping sorrows, e'vn
The flow'r of France—or chivalry or clerks—
Now lean all limp and cankered quite to lace,
For they misdoubt their God and thus all else

Of being, less'ning throne and altar through
A wormling's scoff or rustic masquerade.
        Though France's fire of faith should seem extinct—
Her virtue all to seek—there yet upspear
Those western sons of Lewis, saint and lord
Of Montfort, who their parents' fallows put
To waving wheat of grace. True sons and strong
Of France they stand, or lords or peasants, plight
Of Lewis unto God's Anoint, and bound
In very brotherhood. Confiding in
Thy pierced and burning Phare, I beg how they
Might cheerly take and urge th' redeeming Cross
Against death's dropping engine and ... [*She continues
in silent ecstasy.*]

THE DEMON

                    [*Interrupting.*] Reprieves
Be none! As do, the Heav'n-sought pledge is none.
We'll drown such feathered expectations, clip
The Phoenix hope. What help, these ignorant stobs?
If France shall be a foughten field, it shall
Be sole a punished mortar where the blood
Of pestled kings shall tributary run
To cruddle with the paltry gore and gross
Of beaten peasants, both handsful milled alike
To stimulate, perhaps to medicine, our
Licentious sway. Rawhead and Bloodybones
Shall haunt the leaping hearts of men. Know this,
Dread king, that whatso words I forge and file
To make a meaning—these or other shapes
And timbres, sure as ay you shine a saint
And vex these dwindled eyestones shut or blind

(I scarce know which), tomorrow's death, and you
Nor other may deny the chastisement
Ordained and ineludible. All good,
Show tears who will, must soon be hearsed in greed,
Which men will cense and rev'rence for a god.
Zoolatry returns tricked out in cant
Of brother's love. (A brother shall be known
As by the superciliary brand
Of yore.) Whereat, we ply the knotted scourge
Across a welt'ring sea of shrieks. That flag
Now pure and dropt with flow'rs of gold shall soon
Be draggled foul and dropt with clots of gore.

 Full far from fixing men together, this
Lax love—in very sooth our devil's love
Of self—for being merely felt, not willed,
Shall cause the corporate stones of christly France—
Oh, word unmeant that pulls a rav'ning spate
Of fire through this writhing waste!—shall cause
Those stones to fly apart in bristling, high
Rebellion, to itself each stone become
A narrow law and jealous whereunto
The old authority's become a thing
That flicks infallibly upon the raw,
That ancient edifice of France reduced
To shards and broken rubble—sweepings to
Be brushed by Cyclopean tyrannies
To Hell and terrors inenarrable.

 Hell's weasand's still hawked clear and ready; but
Before we goats may batten huger yet
Upon earth's ghostly offal and before
Our flagellating minions here may spend
Them white in energumen's riot on

The ruddy backs of France, the cross-crowned head
Requires our tend'rest ministrations. First,
His orbed brow we'll duly orb again
With enemies to sap his mobile mind
And farce it with confusion, therewithal
To freeze his backward heart—which measures ta'en
His Frankish head we'll straightaway strike off!
When th' ancient corporations shall become
But stiff'ning corpses—all their ghostly dint
Assumed unto the Revolution—a wretch
Spoiled thiswise clean of all allegiances
Shall stand immediate and naked fore
The long, tentacular, and ready reach
Of greedy usurpation. Know that he
Will now have been conducted to our feast,
Where leaning tables tow'r with fulsome cates
And bowls of poison wash.
　　　　　　　　　　　　Now having put
At France with zeal, we'll visit lands beyond
With ev'ry kind of teen and trouble till
With tonguing up the nations like a press
Of thirsting lions round the muddled hole,
We overtake the utmost of the world
And let exultant gnarls and ululus
Of victory.

St. Lewis IX

　　　　　　　　Pray rein and breathe this jade
Of jactance false as vile; thou'lt prick him till
He drop. Thou jump'st him o'er th' homely rails
Of fact and spur'st him into Faerie.
For in the darkness of thyself thou own'st
That howsoever hardly thou and thine

Shall dare to meet th' almighty Will, y'are quite
As doomed as long since damned. And whereaway
The tale may lead, you cannot not perish France
For ay…

The Demon

      Her flesh we'll hook and pull it from
The bones.

St. Lewis IX

      … or holy Church. When once shall give
The chastisement, the event of all the tears
Long let shall be the flourishment of France,
Her flesh redeemed of the incarnate Word
And by Him lilied fairer than the vales
Of Canaan. Hellish nightjar, tuneless bird,
Throw her a look, who kneels in orison
Yonside our clam'rous striving; say if thou
Needst more than half a greenshot eye to see
That those her pray'rs are quite within the ear
Of God on high, Who loves t'incline Him to
His holy ones and yield Him to the siege
They lay, and wouldst thou nurse the stillborn doubt
That fastly nighs that hallowed hour when thou
And thine shall briefly thrash beneath *Her* heel
And still for ay in limp quietus? Wall
Those bloody eyes and show the horrid world
Those fangs and grinders till thy ugsome lips
Thou cramp, thou knowest well, deceiving bug,
How thou hast heard but truth from these blest lips.

The Demon

And from my flick'ring tongue, O king, take spat
Defiance! Truth's a blade of steel that cleaves
Me through from cap to fork. Deliver me
From thought! I have in evil purpose sole
To hate the edifice of being, whence,
Though I be vised in crack-bone torments and
Devoured of ever-famished flames, I do
My might to warp and wither souls by dint
Of whispering the worm of blandishment
Till judgment strew them down as sudden wind
The blasted orchard drops.
       [*Pointing to his lids.*] These little skins
I'll draw; [*Stopping his ears.*] I'll put these tufted
porches to.
    Thou'rt clean of me, saint king, and I of thee—
And her. Oh, horrifying goodness! Split
Thy blackest muzzle wide, O Hell my home,
Till I escape this terror-freighted verge
Of halidom and like a thunderstone
Down drop me to the cacotopia
That roars and writhes within thy belly's close.

[*Exit.*]

St. Margaret Mary Alacoque

And has our dogged visitor withdrawn?

St. Lewis IX

Ev'n now I saw the wretched trundletail
That tongues a peevish word at whom it flies.

In short, his spirit's quavering liver plucked
And piecemealed forth to sight by fear though he
Had wrapped him round in dudgeon's prickly weeds,
He took his leave, departing netherwards,
Where wait his fellow-damned impatient, I
Should safely say, t' accord seditions 'gainst
The mystical œconomy of grace.

St. Margaret Mary Alacoque

It thus requires to pray. With ev'ry zeal
Of humblehearts repair we to our Queen
And Mother intercessory enthroned
And blest above seraphic joys. Against
Our purpose to Her throne of light hard by
The Session of Her Son, pray sphere we full
Our endless bedes with hope and wreathe them round
That we might cast them surely on Her care,
Who may repose our hearts' rogations in
The dazzling furnace of the Sacred Heart.

[*Exeunt.*]

Scene 2

[*A meeting of the Council of Dispatches (Dépêches) at Marly on June 19, 1789, the King presiding. James Necker, Director of the Treasury, is finishing the reading of his memorandum on his recent proposal of a* séance royale *to address the organisation of the Estates General, which opened on May 5 previous.*]

Necker

These presents, then, so throughly aired, if giv'n
The sovran nod of Majesty, may we
Not see, and soon, good Sire of all in France
That hope and you, my fellow gentlemen,
A Session Royal wherein a country may
Be cobbled to by reasoned compromise?
In sum, the Third Estate, a creature of
The King, Who spoke it forth to sober down
The greater clerks and nobles self-besot,
Shall like th' amphibious Hydra put forth full
As many heads again as now they field
And have that, what shall bear upon the good
Of France entire, the three estates as by
A metamorphosis shall melt and merge,
As t'were, to vote by head. Thus commoners
May bear away the bell by simple tale
Of noses spite of lineage long and reach
Of higher orders that should loom as large as
Old Leviathan. Contrariously,
For aughtsoever that shall aughtways touch
On feudal rights and rights ecclesial,
By order shall they vote, tricam'ral and
Discrete. Thus, lords and prelates leagued may bear
The plaited crown though commoners out-teem
The silvern shoals that dart athwart the deep.
By this may be preserved the rights and rule
Of Holy Church and glorious blood, of France
As much a hard, high pillar each, I say,
As ever was the Common Third of men.

[The King, followed by the ministers, rises to leave as a valet enters and whispers in His ear.]

Count de Montmorin

Long miles of toil and weary days, if I
May dare reflection, our now well-breathèd minds
Have worn. Were matters else, I would but sink
Mine own within the deepest down of sleep.
As matters are, I would but mount and spur
Unto my goodwife's bed of pain to fan
Her hectic brow, her measled limbs t'anoint.

King Lewis XVI

A pitiable tale, indeed! Did We
Not cite thee hence to serve the weal of France?
Sh' has need, good sir. Pray leave thy faintish spouse
To leechcraft. Let Aesclepius breech the vein.
Attend Our soon return, good gentlemen.

[Exit the King.]

Count de la Luzerne

Why, man, thou spak'st a thoughtless speech. As if
His Majesty in council suffered more
Than the affairs of State to be within
His hearing! Worse again, the Dolphin, Prince
Enthroned within his father's bleeding heart
Lies two weeks gathered to the sleeping kings
Of eld ev'n like a ruddied rosebud lipped
Farewell and beaded over with a dew
Of father's tears, a costly chrism 'gainst

The Resurrection. Therewithal, what recks
The Nation recks the King or night or day;
'Twas ever this: no king puts off the cap
Of iron care. The maintenance of France
Scarce grants a pillow unto kingly eyes
That burn with grief. A jealous mistress, she.

Count de Montmorin

My childish prating quite outran the pace
Of solemn prudence. 'Pon this thoughtless head
Ye saw me bring the weight condign of all
His Majesty's much-wonted brusquerie.

Necker

Come, come; this contretemps is quite as naught.
The King is called away, my Lords, by whom
If not the Queen right as our Sovran made
To set His seal on this our shifting of
These plaguesome, thrice-insuff'rable Estates.

Count de Montmorin

Pray tell, my Lord, were we misled to think
You champion of the great estates, those eggs
That with your brooding once may hatch and fledge
A parliament to rival England's own?

Necker

My gale of words were sole the venting of
A spleen much wrought upon these several weeks.
Now, to the point. The air of minds new-met
Has come unspelled; our moment's milk of bliss

Now spoils upon the tongue or ere it may
Be gulped. That younger brother to the King
Has doubtless gained the Queen's new-pliant mind
Though She till lately bare the Third avault
A lily hand. His Highness will have kings
Unbridled save by jig of God or yerk
Of ancient use, for whose eximious blood
The Third's a thing should lie asleep, slack-lipped
In poppy fumes not less than ever—to sprawl
An eighth forgotten 'mongst the sleepers i'
Th' Ephesian cave. How long these months I sat
A beggar plying th' instant dish before
The royal gates of indecision! Sure,
The obolus of compromise I won
Has slipped my feeble grasp and sings in gay
Derision 'long the pavement of a hard
Reality. I maunder. Lords of France,
Do all may bring the King to compromise
Lest France be harrowed up and sown with salt.
To them would straightway bound and spur to ride
The thirdlings down, I say 'twere better far
To tender forth such willing heart as may
Appease and balm their reasonable wants.
    Ah well, along the shaded the green without,
Where Progne spends her ardent melodies
Upon the even's air, may we not find
A moment's gale to sweep the spangled brow?

[*Exeunt omnes.*]

Scene 3

[Enter the King. From across the stage, enter the Queen, followed by the Count of Artois.]

GUARD

The King!

KING LEWIS XVI

Pray, Ma'am, what matter's toward that needs Our swift
Translation hither? Know the Council—wan
And peaking—waits upon Our pleasure yet.

QUEEN MARY ANTOINETTE

The matter—one of highest moment, Sire—
Is e'en that composition of th' Estates,
Wherein till now Your Majesty, imbow'red
With all Your ministers, has long been merged
More deep than dryad in the rooted tree.
Defer decision yet a little till
We ask, both Monseigneur and I, how You
As from the heaving flag would captain and
Dispose th' Estates, afloat and blown athwart?

KING LEWIS XVI

Sweet wife to all Our nobler wishes, blood
Of Ours and dear, know how these weeks Our care
Is caution, how from ev'ry march and verge
We needs must look the looming matter hard
And hearken ev'ry thinking voice about.

Queen Mary Antoinette

But Lewis, hast thou not of ministers
A score at least before thee summoned by
The pair that e'en as it were sport must close
Like gladiators measuring spoken swords
Day long o'er one or other shapen clay
Of government, each image mirror of
A mind imperious? Is there issue yet
Of these logomachies?

King Lewis XVI

        In sooth, my Heart,
A moth of doubt still gnaws the weft of all
My thinking. Though I own how I delight
To number ev'ry leaf along the bine
Of ramifying facts, for me 'tis rare
T'invent the terminating pod that drops
Within the fertile mind the bean of sweet
Decision. But in greater sooth, what recks
It how th' Estates are formed and marshaled? Were
Th' Estates of heretofore not diversly
Arranged, proceeding differently, as pleased
The genius of the hour and circumstance?

The Count of Artois

O father throned o'er France and crowned, meseems
The genius of this hour's impiety.
The Third but now made bold enough to style
Itself the National Assembly, pinned
Cockade of impudence.

King Lewis XVI

'Tis but a phrase.

Queen Mary Antoinette

A phrase that soughs sedition through the oaks
Of ancient France, so please Your Majesty.

The Count of Artois

By flourish of a resolution, they
Have roundly given France to know that hence
The present wise of raising taxes stands
Without the law, by which fair sleight they stand
Themselves without the law, who had no pow'r
T'ordain, except as by a thimblerig
Wherein the thimble Third enclosed the plump
Pea jurisdiction. Is this thimble not
A pod would drop upon the fertile mind
The seed of burgeoning decision sweet?

King Lewis XVI

Give ear now, dear self-sorbèd brother Ours,
Now brought abubble by combustion of
Events, wherefore, We ask, whenso a tax
Shall be proposed, should not Our Third Estate,
Whose bounden do was e'er to pay whatso
Was put upon their shriv'ling purse, have say
In wise of him that pays the piper? Let
Them call the tune, say We. So say shouldst thou.

The Count of Artois

Though farming publicans dun peasants ne'er
So greedily, this Third, O Sire, aswim
As 'tis with impious Philosophes, should not,
I beg to say, be loosed on Christian France,
Who floats within their soulless eyes as so
Much ravin, not alone as property,
But too as flesh and blood of ancient use,
Which they would shark away till she be left
A rack of osseous abstraction.

King Lewis XVI

                    Strange
These words from one whose soul's hard mould has yet
To bloom such violet remorse for sin
As on the morning of a soul astir
The Christ asperses with His rorid Grace.
For all thy head may chord thee son'rous with
The mind of Holy Church, thy heart at loose
Has downward haled thee to the turbid deeps
Where lashes all the mucinous welter of
Illicit love, the weed that waits to foul
The sunken self. Dear brother, thou'rt not whole.

[*Enter two members of the Parliament of Paris.*]

First Parliamentarian

Your Majesty, our Liege Lord King, within
The Third th' ensewerèd enemies of France
Are now conflate; their exhalations waft
The land across to breed distempers strange,

Which render the receptive out of whole
Conceit with France as she is: the sum of all
She has been. They fancy how the country's come
A category of the mind spilled void
Of substance only to be freighted full
Of suppositious dreams, which now become
A kind of sovran crown fore which the world
Unwashed must bend the humbled knee else feel
It smashed as by a mace of absolute
Prerogative—the Gen'ral Will, to wit,
Their own, more sweet and madding more than ev'n
That mel made mad of deadly aconite.

Second Parliamentarian

As to the Third Estate, we subjects of
The very Crown ask that His Majesty
Misdeem them not this day, misdoubt them more;
Misdoers are they most, whose actions give
Them proud and prone to wrest His sovranty.

King Lewis XVI

These words fetch echoes from the long-ago
Of loyalties twixt lord and man. Whate'er,
Right hon'rables, the words rehearsed from far,
Sound not all echoes hollow? Shall We not
Recall how when forth ev'ry coin of France
Within the ear of herald's throat We bade
Her notables forthwith t'attend upon
Our presence, these when all forgathered with
Their Sovran and invited to put off,
This crying nonce, that close-wove habit hight

Self-interest and assume such taxes as
Should help the fisc from penury and ease
The burthen staggering the peasant, cried
As with a single tongue "*non possumus*."
    Then ye, longsighted of Our parliaments,
Not less shown gripple of prerogative
[*Aside to the Queen.*] (Nor less meseems but lickpennies
near all),
    Your very selves, as vigilant as geese,
Looked black upon a like proposal that
To full the purse of State it needs to prune
The brakes and thickets of exemptions sown
To serve the exigent hour now here now there
Through centuries till royal governance
At last was compromised and rendered null.
Ye come in feather of a vassal, but
The fox's tail withal We spy behind.
For lest ye sanction this malod'rous plea,
Ye durst to claim yourselves incompetent
To grant a tax, averring that th' Estates
Alone were herein competent, which said,
We thereupon aroused and called the Three.
And now, these same—say rather that unlick'd
Estate of commoners, with helmets horn'd—
Stands fair to raid your fine acropolis
And swallow in your duties whole, drink off
Unceremonious your pow'rs nor scarce
A thank-you belched. And who may blame your care,
Who stand to be superfluous? Whereat,
'Tis Our Estates with whom We must confer,
As you implied, or do We here misdeem?

[*Enter Cardinal de la Rochefoucauld and Mgr. Le Clerc de Juigné, Archbishop of Paris.*]

Lord Cardinal, dear cousin, and thou good
Archbishop, are you come in cause with these?

CARDINAL DE LA ROCHEFOUCAULD

God grant His Christian Majesty all grace
That, reached to Him from Heaven's height by Her
Most amiable, our Mother undefiled
And veiled with most exalt humility,
May cause Him well to serve the State and well
To save the Church. Upon His nointed head
Pray fall and fast God's choicest blessings so
He keep His oath to holy God, Whom all
We pray He'll love above all else till death
Sweep round the blade and send His soul to scale.

KING LEWIS XVI

May angel ministers stay up thy hands,
Great soul, at prayer ever for this realm.
We cannot but incline to all thou'st come
To word; thy ev'ry word is plain and blest.

CARDINAL DE LA ROCHEFOUCAULD

[*Kneeling at the King's feet, followed by the Archbishop.*]
Your Majesty, our surety, by month
And morbid month since You in flow'r put on
The sacred person of a king agone
These fifteen years, Yourself, the Kingdom self,
And Holy Church, so haughtily contempt

By them that scorn authority, have been
The subject of a frank assault. A swarm
Of busy men and base with venom flown
And tapped of ready stings still bombinate
Both out and in a skep of closely wov'n
Sedition.

King Lewis XVI

      Well We know what hive thy eyes
So nettles; 'tis the Palais Royal, seat
Of cousin Orleans, the shadow France.

Cardinal de la Rochefoucauld

And shade to all the thirsting kind that pant
For philosophic fuddlement within
A blushing crystal brimmed with flattering lies,
None headier than the claim, most virtuous
The man that bridles least the ready blood
Of mettled nature, evil sejant like
A blazoned beast not in the heart of man
But only in the dented scutcheon of
The institutions of his making. What
May wait the Crown, what wait the country, Sire,
When irreligion such as this besots
The new-blown flow'r of France? A notion of
This like must string the thews of Christendom,
Make parasites of priest and prince alike,
And quickly reave the multitude of men
Of probity and sure the pearl of Faith.
This lie and other like intoxicate
Th' unholy Third, who will be cast to do

Your Majesty no good; both halidom
And Holy Church they cordially hate.

Mgr. Le Clerc de Juigné

[*Pointing to all suppliants except the Cardinal.*]
So please Your Majesty, these here but give
The factions as they are; put not their words
Away. They only wish . . .

King Lewis XVI

                        How know you all
These things, my Lords? In truth, but now We felt
Th' immensurable world beneath Us move.

Cardinal de la Rochefoucauld

Defend religion, Sire, in the name
Of good St. Lewis and the piety
Of Your august forebears. Embattle now
Your lilied crown against the wolving of
Your foes confederate. God man it with
The Angel Guardian of France! Flash forth,
Good Majesty, the glancing sword of State,
The singing tongue of steel that quails at once
The stomach proud! O tender not these men
At enmity with France and Christ Himself!

[*Enter Mme. de Polignac wheeling in the royal children
(the Dauphine, Mary Theresa Charlotte (Madame Royale),
and the Dauphin, Lewis Charles); the Queen pushes the
children into the arms of the King.*]

Queen Mary Antoinette

Pray do away Your hesitation as
You cherish ev'n Our little spray of buds
So lately culled by Heaven; do Your pain,
My Lord, to flick the canker inching nigh.
I give for granted, heart and husband Ours,
How at this present men are met to hatch
Such sinuous wiles as may ere long mischieve
The family; as well We fear that soon
The day may be when people's goodly kin
To God will be their crime, that those devout
Will blench in time and bleed 'neath scorpion, screws,
And scourge, once more to seed with blushing rills
Of charity the fallows of the realm.

King Lewis XVI

From thee and them I'll take tuition, thou
My heart's repose. I will not more reluct.
    Ye set Us tasks, good gentles, and We take
Them to Our heart, which Heaven plate with steel
Of bright resolve and wreathe with aureole
Of gold and lilies' double nod! Produce
Monsieur; a Council We convene—upon
This present. Let th' Estates each bend itself
Obedient to its several chamber, there
T' recall its duties to the realm! Now keep
A care who peril France and Holy Church!

Cardinal de la Rochefoucauld

God save the King!

King Lewis XVI

God save the soul of France!

[*Enter a chamberlain.*]

Chamberlain

Your Majesty, the Council Room stands wide.

[*Exit the chamberlain, followed by the King, followed by everyone else according to rank.*]

Scene 4

[*Enter the King with James Necker.*]

Guard

The King!

Necker

And will Your Majesty, as You resolved,
That deputies shall each one ply him sole
Within the chamber of his equals, there
As prelate, lord, or burgess modestly
To serve the realm or feel the rod outraged?
'Twere late, meseems, to put a burden on
A beast as restive as the Third, become
A colt to patience and docility.

King Lewis XVI

So said We, sir, yes'treen. It then seemed clear
The matter's moment asked an action, but
A doubt like morning's mask of fog has rolled
Upon Our waking countenance. We would
Keep fair with ev'ry of Our children; it
Requires to pacify the instant tear,
The warrantable plaint. Deaf-minded would
We never rule. Permit them met conjoint—
Abstract from wont and way of life—to try
Out true from false, approving levies, loans,
Nor less the in and out of th' pocket royal,
All things may bear upon the gen'ral weal.
But mind, no motion carries save at least
Two pompous wigs in three shall give the yea.
Indeed, estates provincial We would grant.

Necker

His Majesty will kindly give me leave
To ransom from astonishment such scrag
Of breath as may croak joy at His so bold,
So politic relentment. Compromise:
Is't not, Your Majesty, confession of
Reality, a … ?

King Lewis XVI

Sir, We wish to be
As large to these as to the seed of Our
Begetting. Are We not the father of
Them all? We give to God above this night
The morrow Session Royal. Be it in
His constant care. 'Tis time to summon sleep.

[*Exeunt.*]

ACT 2

Scene 1

[*A salon in the Palais Royale, Paris, seat of the House of Orleans. Enter Lewis Philip, Duke of Orleans, the Countess de Coigny, M. Adrian Duport, other guests, and members of the Duke's retinue.*]

COUNTESS DE COIGNY

[*Addressing one of the guests.*]
The Queen, my Lord? In silks and diamonds
On high She billows large and thwart the sun
That fulls th' initiate mind with mystic beam.
She shadows o'er the People, doomed by this
To miserable nescience—chained, trod down,
And rudely wronged. And to Her wedded King,
Whom still She has in high contempt, She proves
No better make than she-wolf feeding foul
Upon the hapless hearts of men, each throne
Of beating sentiment its dish of blood.
The sounded name of such a dam appalls
The crims'ning ears of shamefast decency.
A pox upon the patched and painted sow!

AN AGED GUEST

[*Addressing the Duke of Orleans.*]
Your Highness, but she cease she must mischieve

The Queenly name not sole to quality
But even to the bookless mob, whose pot
Of late is heady rumour and whose meat
Is what may touch a burnished name. They farce
Them with such offal till their bellies strut
With slander and detraction e'vn as this.
Pray how may lies and malediction speed
Our noble purpose unto liberty,
Equality, and fair fraternity?

The Duke of Orleans

My man, what time did boggling ninnies e'er
Convey a shining dream to finished deed?
Nay, muliebral curses help, my Lord;
The scorpion tongue inspires a furious dance
Along the squalid alleys of Montmartre,
Whilst raising wales along the Sovran's back.
She bends her tongue to loose a barbed lie,
'Tis true; but truer 'tis that lies may serve
Our good, identical, be't said, with that
Of France.

An Aged Guest

Bring argument, great Prince, I beg,
For all hortation this side havoc howled.
I hear a fearsome logic in your words;
It lifts the aged hairs upon my neck.

The Duke of Orleans

Give aged ear: I tell thee of a truth,
In furtherance of our design I stand

Indifferent though it need for Frenchmen to
Be stark suggested to barbarities.
From tinder cured is fetched seditious fire.

AN AGED GUEST

What may possess a man so fiercely thus
To breathe?

THE DUKE OF ORLEANS

      Grey hairs, or starting stiff or flat
Asleep, will not absolve temerity,
My Lord, nor shall our cause forgive a qualm.
We must upon the quarry King gain all
The ground we may till driven hard to ground
He yield the Cap of State, become our prized
Attire of many-tinèd flowers de luce.
Keep fair with us and prosper, else from fort
To feeble gone, thou be like—someone—damned
For indecision.
[*Referring him to a waiter carrying a tray.*]
      Take a cordial.
  Monsieur Duport, how proves our smithery
To heat and bend the minds of hobnails, lords,
And burgesses along the stolid land?

DUPORT

Nine bales of cendiary broadsheets set
Upon two drays and veiled, Your Highness, will
This secret night be pulled by snorting brawn
Through th' iron-studded jaws set wide below,
Which then will stand a gaping oracle

That though possessed and blind shall by those tongues
Of paper multiplied arouse the French
From their oppressive sleep and slavery.

The Duke of Orleans

These flights pray save for speeches from the bench.
More's yet to 'complish. It requires that all
Well-seen in wielding words—and nothing loath
To dirt their garments—come and, doing coy
Reserve away, sharp swift their pens and put
Them to with bigger zeal than yet has squeezed
The bellows o'er the human coals of France
(Who live in hope of manumission). Though
That freight of rhetoric that waits upon
The cobblestones below will do its good
Far yond the Palace gates, we need such men
For urging of the cause as set alight
Their grains of incense fore the Furies. Such
A one I have in mind … And where he comes!

[*Enter John Paul Marat. (The player who portrays this
character should be recognisable as the person who portrayed
the demon at the beginning of the play.)*]

    Monsieur Marat, thou'rt kind indeed to grace
This glad occasion with such presence as
Must soon convict the world of how thou lov'st
The noble kind, I say—of shackled man.

MARAT

[Bowing.]
Receive my bent esteem, high Prince. What man
Would dare gainsay your hieratic word?

THE DUKE OF ORLEANS

At twitting I should run a tilt had we
A larger gift from miserable time.
To be at but a whispered word, pray know
Thou'rt here, fair friend, to be enlisted in
A happy band all met to cite the blood
Of men to fervid action. Thirty told
Of th' Brethren we have scattered broadcast o'er
This mould of France, who at this present knit
Both bone and sinew of a sleeping sprawl
Of flesh, the fierce, titanic flower that
We name the Revolution, soon to reach
Its crimsoned hand to cull the golden sun.
This giant whenas set upon its legs
Will be a simple calf and surd. Wherefore,
'Tis thou must be its vibrant cords of speech;
'Tis thou must sometime be its brain, withal.
    Strike in with us, I say! For so thou join
Us thou'lt have free approach not sole to us
But other also that can speed thee and
Thy patriotic stir. From hence in time
With our unfolding, full thy feather's throat
With wine and vitriol, that scribbling what
May flush the mind with roseate dreams and fires
Of indignation, thou with us may but
A day or twain from this make fair the road

To revolution. Pray, did I misthink
Thou'dst have the tooth and stomach for the deeds
In ink that must be done? With thy black milk
Thou must be passing gen'rous at the pail.

MARAT

No need to dare the simple child, O great
Of millions. Know me milch enough and more
That giving down white truth, or black, I should
Not fail to suckle ev'ry Gallic slave
In fetters forged. Well found with will this head,
As stark and cool as heart of demon damned.
With hungry expectation, I accept
As from the People this sweet mead and wide
Of clover and shall shortly be at grass.
The clotted beestings men shall pull of me
Will set an edge to their desires that, when
We shall break off their iron gyves, they'll bolt
Like slav'ring dogs to find the silkened leg,
The throat with falling bands or lace endued.
To all I shall delight to throw upon
The cringing page I'll put a bitter point
Till indignation swoll'n and finding last
A universal voice reply like shot
From Belgium to the Province. How I hate
All them enchaired above us, kings and all
Their coroneted rats, their mitred scum!

THE DUKE OF ORLEANS

Quite so. From folds of secrecy we'll draw
And stick them to the helve! E'er then thou'rt sure,

Marat, to do us all delirious!

MARAT

A day is planned for death, I see; the milk
Of blood will sop the thirsting fallows soon.
So be it. All must howl who dare t'oppress
The People. Who, and howso many, at
This sentence should reluct must patient lie—
As loathsome traitors to Humanity—
Beneath a heavy brand and sharp of shame.
For at a thought, I say, grim greyhound brute
Resolve, espying any stirring of
Compassion, must give chase and strike it like
A bawling rabbit, worrying it limp.
This night be flint all honest hearts, from which
The hammerstrokes of iron tyranny
May scatter angry sparks ambitious in
The monstrous magazine of rankling swoll'n
In hearts of humbled backs and doubled fists!
    I go to set the world upon its wig.
About the mews of thoroughbreds I'll buzz
A biting legsticker to Court and King.

THE DUKE OF ORLEANS

So please thee, give the King as one perplexed,
The Queen as grasping and extravagant.
Of aught we spake no whisper, need I say?

Marat

Hearsed here our words nor never echoed more!
[*Offering his hand, the Duke recoiling.*]
Strike brisk we then our hands upon it. Ha!
This scabid rind new risen from the bath
Would brush you harmless, sir. Be long of life!

[*Exit.*]

Duport

What more this man than snapping trundletail,
Your Highness? How may we here forth entrust
Our fortunes to the squint and stripe that wrung
But now the tribute of offended eyes?
Sure, as he rudely span about and stalked
Through crowd and door the evening air to vex
Your guests as one fet deep a sigh of ease.

The Duke of Orleans

A cur of parts this man, Monsieur Duport,
A never-winded harrier whom we
Shall slip as pleases us. And what though he
Should foam about the chops? Our need, nor less,
Be sure, is energumens such as this
We pleased to entertain this even soft.

Duport

But how with our so nicely builded plans
Can he be aughtways made compliable?
Be, sir, premonished, he will not away
With place or worth, or late or soon. It turns

The mind to contemplate how with his sleight
Of quill, from which he knows to draw all words
As may strike up into the head, he'll get
In men a bloody-minded animus
Not sole against your cousin King, but you
As well, a Prince of the Blood, confess you ne'er
So much devoted to equality.

THE DUKE OF ORLEANS

What smote thee spang upon the mind but now,
Monsieur, was just a doing man and bold,
If something froward—one of us; he knows
Us for a brother, history and blood
Abjuring. Habile yond his scribbling peers
This stick at spurring on the panting heart.
Might not he fair be named the greatest of
A man that e'er a rabble roused? A man
To wild a world were not to say awry.

DUPORT

Y'are taken with him quite; no words, my Lord,
Of mine will carry home; they're nothing in
Your hearing. But we've cast to do away
The ancient wonts and should noway take shame.
Th' event of all this do may scarce be guessed.

    So instantly has present business plied
Upon my bended back that I have gone
Without a crust of time to ask what saw
You at the Session Royal this merry morn?

The Duke of Orleans

In secret joy this day my gaping orbs
Were feasted to a royal failure bald
And to the backbone. First, the simpleton
In full regalia, scepter, crown, and hand
Of justice, to th' Assembly rolled at long
His royal way, on either side whereof
Stood throngs as quiet as the growing grass,
Their quiv'ring hopes beneath the iron tyres
Laid flat. (How clever Mirabeau to name
This silence wroth the school of kings!) Enthroned
Before th' assembled and immingled states,
The King showed how a mind had sicked and died,
For straight a drop of words fell stillborn from
His bellied lips. But ere He triced a breath
To speak, indeed or ere He darked the door
Put wide for His approach, His minions new
And pitiably naïve had blazed for all
The programme of the King, wherein was writ,
"The King doth will," a form till now unthought.
Not he that liked his person to the sun
Was heard in governance to say, "We will."
At such a whip-crack e'en the nobles jibbed,
The very men should reap the Session clean
Of benefit. Suffice it, friend, to say
To men of unreceptive mind the King
Addressed His speech. Where fain He gave the purse
Of France to the Assembly, loosed the tongues
And pens of who would say their minds, He then
Took mad adieu of plain reality
And bade disperse forthwith th' assembled, 'pon
The morrow morn each man enjoined to take

Him smartly to the chamber lotted him.
    On this our Mirabeau averred how save
At point of bayonet no wise should they
Be turned like cattle to the chambers three.
Th' immortal rose on Hebe's silken cheek
Would give and go ere men as these should slink
Away once more to feel the iron round
Their necks, once more to fall a-jarring one
With other. Sir, the Session periled Him;
The King's no longer reachless. Clear as glass,
His presence perished much His hold on men's
Allegiance. Spurring deep, to earth we'll drive
Him soon. From now, Marat will have Him in
A tale with Attila and Genghis Khan!
In short th' unhappy King, like folly's self,
His Cap of State become a cap of bells,
His scepter now a bauble, pulls a face
And prates like Merry-Andrew.
                              Night has worn
His weary way to cradled morn; the guests
Have bidden to the Marchioness their stiff
Adieus. 'Tis time we shuttlecocked our own.

DUPORT

Until the morrow morn, when we'll again
To boot and horse! Is not the horse we sit
Each day our Revolution rough, than which
No wilder broomtail snorts on the Camargue?

[*Exeunt.*]

ACT 3

Scene 1

[*On the heights above Paris, enter respectively from the left and right a sentry of one of the King's regiments and a gentleman of the King's hunting party in the vicinity.*]

SENTRY

Now stand! And say who lives.

GENTLEMAN

                    The King, foraye.

SENTRY

And what, sir, seek ye, come at cockcrow 'pon
These lonely purlieus? Foxes here be few.

GENTLEMAN

About the pleasure of the King I go,
Whose pleasure 'tis this rorid hour of spring
To ride at large and, finding out the fox,
To wand away the tedium and toil
Of kingcraft. Both we wait upon His beck,
Not less, my man, the royal foxes yond
That vale, whereof one head less canny than
Its kin shall from the royal wainscot stare

For trophy to this morning's boist'rous hunt.

SENTRY

The King is nigh then. Spur and breathe You well,
Good King! And rule as fits the golden right
By God set gleaming on Your serene brow!
My Lord, 'tis plain to wearied eyes atop
This vantage high, where th' angry ensign strains
And snaps at ev'ry wind that bustles through,
How fair that misty vale now shimmers 'neath
The smiling magnanimity of dawn,
Whiles at a throw of eyes to left there smites
This harried heart the smoke and yearning spires
Of Paris. Now and then, my Lord, meseems
There floats to ear th' iron-sung dirge of tow'r
And steeple, weeping dissolution's wave.

GENTLEMAN

Ah shriftless Paris, torn as 'tis and spread
Beneath our augur's eyes, shows ominous
Her winding ways; that glist'ring night that turned
Above us minutes since disast'rous shone.
For when the troubles first became, that is
When needs the King spake forth the Three Estates,
Then all the vanities—those dragon's teeth
By Satan sown along the hearts of men—
Sprang armed and ready, soon confederate
For spoil. Thou know'st, as will the world ere long,
How when the King conceded spacious pow'rs
Of legislation to th' assembled, He
Required how hence they should disperse and straight

Resume their ancient hierarchy, who,
As one, then gave immediate tongue and split
Their angry throats. At which the heedful King
Relented. Now wrapt round in somber cloak
Of sanctimony, glorious withal
In greed beneath, they gaze the waiting wealth
Of Paris, th' ancient lands and treasures of
The Church, the royal palaces—all claimed
Of them for coming confiscation. All
These heads are but a horse that will not rein.

SENTRY

But sure the King, this son of Charlemagne,
Of sainted Lewis, they will yet respect.

GENTLEMAN

True, many are who love the King yet think
Him an impedient to their pow'r and brag.
Now worship and affection trend away
To cooler climes of bloodless thought. There breathe
Above the artic line some few as cold
As Cain, nay, puritanic Goneril.
Without th' Assembly other some make cause
With scours of ink against the King. The Queen's
Good name they scandal fore the mob and all
Within the ears of everywhere. There drifts
Across the land a ceaseless rataplan
Of lies and slander. Nor the Church is spared.

SENTRY

The King's a withy man, my Lord, a tough
And flexible; no brittle twig is He.
Who blow upon a gentlewoman's name,
Who lour and make to blackguard holy Church,
Are faitors foul and cowards fell; and I
Much think how they must put them hard within
The awful danger of the King. Myself
And thirty thousand soldiers more are poised
Upon these heights, where should those impious rogues
Aforesaid dare put Paris to the sack,
Full deep we shall be ranked and sword-in-hand
Be rayed across this rolling grass to wait
Our crowned Commander's nod, which dropt, a bleak
And bristling multitude, both horse and foot,
Will forth in close formation move as one
Upon the prisoned city. Woe to all
Have plotted ruin to the realm! Who scape
The ball and bayonet, 'tis sure, shall prove
Upon the bloody block a painful end.

GENTLEMAN

My faith has given me that, by the grace
Of God, the King will never break His eyes
Away from duty, stern soever it
Should sometime prove. Than He, nathless, but few
Are they that stand in starker need of pray'r,
For He must thwart the bloody-minded crew
At enmity with God and Crown, hence stay
The billowing titan breathing bloody smoke
From greenly should'ring o'er the bulwark reas'n

And sheeting 'cross the bubbling face of France
Without a breath beneath a world unknown—
In fine, the Revolution must undo.
The King it is must save the dark'ning day,
Except it simply be the day of France
Is setting; gentrice not avails, 'tis sure,
Nor yet 'twould seem, an honest yeomanry.
    But days agone within the tripping heart
Of Paris flown with rustics wanting work
And bread—they wished daubed
o'er with trouble—plunged
The vaulting Orleans, who durst engage
A pack of frank hyaenas charged of him
To torch both home and manufactory
Of worthy Réveillon, who late had pled
For low'ring wage, although, be't said, without
Effect on those of his renowned employ.
These fiery deeds the brutes dispatched at once
Whilst region soldiery stood by and gaped.
With pow'rs as this the King contends, Whose crown
They look with all their greedy eyes. Behind
Which glancing veils in secret quite they plan
Their plagues and visitations grim. Wherefore,
The King is stoutly met at ev'ry turn.

SENTRY

In us who step in solemn troop behind
That whitest weft dropt o'er with Heaven's light
Of gold He grasps, my Lord, a gleaming sword
And true, a ready blade with dint and sweep
Enough to fell the monster there astir.
    But lo, except these peel'd eyes play me false,

The King is horsing hither now across
That beaded down. 'Tis time my leave were ta'en.
Long live the King! My Lord, farewell.

Gentleman

                        Godspeed!

[*From the right, enter the King and His retinue, including the Duke de Broglie. From the left, enter the Baron de Besenval, lieutenant colonel commanding the deployed regiments.*]

Sentry

[*Standing apart.*]
The King!

Baron de Besenval

These legions here assembled, Sire, and I
Confess You fealty complete. God shield
Your Majesty's forbearant reign and mild!

King Lewis XVI

And give thee joy, Lord Baron. Loyalty
As thine this heart refreshes. Let us now
Improve the shining hour! As bidden here
By mandate of the Session Royal, sir,
Both thou and these amassed by myriad
These sev'ral weeks stand guardians of peace
Within Our capital below. Or ere
Thou muster horse and foot, await Our word.
Mind well, no order shall We render save
When men raise riot or rebellion fair.

When with Our signal thou have gone amongst
The misbehaved about the city, more
Should not be needed than to crowd them all
Away; school not their backs. We would not war
With Frenchmen, children in Our constant cure.
Immit no urge to jar with makebates; make
All fast thy ears against mere whisperings
And soughs of mad sedition. Reach no blows
Undue, my Lord. Like hounds before the hunt
Awakened men may open long and loud.
Premonish them and bide with rooted legs.

Baron de Besenval

I too, Your Majesty, should still be loath
To make at men of France before, that is,
I should be graced of Your express command.
Far be from me, my Liege, aught urge conceived
Of soldierly ambition rashly to
Put spurs to these Your galliard men-at-arms.
Be caution motto of this sober morn!

King Lewis XVI

We see that from the field of officers
We chose a wheaten kernel, nor a tare
Unapt for this most periled of commands.

Baron de Besenval

His Majesty has honoured me and owned
Me with a jest. God save my King and France!

King Lewis XVI

Our visitation must be brief, my Lord,
As whist. Now come a tonic hour to drive
The foxes ere We dark the door of State!

Baron de Besenval

Pray would His Majesty perchance accept
Against the chill a stirrup cup of tea?

King Lewis XVI

[*Addressing the gentleman.*]
Attend us, sir. Anon we spur away.

[*Exeunt the King and the Baron de Besenval.*]

Sentry

But little was we dreamt, my Lord, whilst we
Were lately peering into birds to see
Their entrails whether clean or queer, that this
We heard, at hearing which I stood fordead,
Was only making here apace. What man
That treasures hearth and hills and having heard
Might stay his eyne from weeping stillicides?

Gentleman

Like yonder fading moon of morn that pulls
The seas now to now fro, man's lurid doubts
And wanton witch away once bold resolve
To make him docile as the current tide.
The way showed fair for compromise, I ween.

[*Enter the King and the Baron de Besenval.*]

King Lewis XVI

[*Addressing the Baron de Besenval.*]
Across the troubled Channel, royal Charles,
Sad cousin gone, my Lord, these hundred years
And fifty, strove to save the English crown
From depredation of his subjects own
By summoning the sword, and for his pains
He lay at length beneath the hooded head
And heard the iron answer of the axe.

Baron de Besenval

But surely, Sire, a sound it was that here
In France will never fetch an echo, for ...

King Lewis XVI

Be that as may, a king should not recourse
To plying weapons with his subject sons.
The blood of Frenchmen must the sinews of
The Nation feed, nor vainly as a spout
Of smoking gore clot thick the ground. Now at
This juncture, sir, Our cure from God is, at
The cramping hand of assiduity,
To fine-draw rents of faction and dispute.
[*Addressing the gentleman.*]
Now fastly, sir, to horse we all and gone!

[*Exeunt the King and His train. Exit the sentry, resuming his watch.*]

ACT 4

Scene 1

[*At the palace of Versailles three months later, enter the King from the right; enter from the left the Count de Saint-Priest, the Marquis de la Tour du Pin, the Prince de Beauveau, and James Necker.*]

Count de Saint-Priest

We cry His Majesty good welcome and
Inquire how fared this mellow morning's shoot.

King Lewis XVI

Whilst moaning trees, strong swayed of winds, besprent
Bright strewments o'er the grave of summer, high
The frighted pheasants rocketed, We urged
Much lead, much birds th' retainers bagged. Now, lords,
To graver matter still; rehearse this morn's
Untoward history. How came this wave
Of women, how this regimented surge
Of soldiery? To Lafayette We deem
They bear obedience, to Us We doubt.

Count de Saint-Priest

The beast of Revolution, having put
Its tusks and grinders up, is now afoot
And bold these three fraught months, Your Majesty,

To answer which, so please You, strive I e'vn
Till now to quit myself a man, and, more,
A constant servant to my sovran King.
    For in his army, crescent Lafayette,
Become the very targe and spear of Mars,
So bulks as to eclipse poor Orleans,
Who overreaching, as a duke agog
To be a king, now breathes, nay puffs, a prince
Unhorsed, unhelped, and soon, I claim, e'en by
His very sleeve-creepers to be forsook
And clean forgot. This Lafayette, at urge
Of these his faithful's instant musket prongs,
Is come right hard upon the dainty heels
Of harridans and men in awkward drape
Of skirts and shawl. All these, long plied of fair
Mendacities and amiable lies,
Require both bread and revolution. On
This morning's road midst leaves in motley through
The haze down-warping, one would cry, "We'll nill
Us nothing; we shall do the Queen away!"
And other would aver, "We'll make Her as
A serpent throw Her jeweled skin." "We'll have
Approach to King and Council or be necked!"
So other still. Which tale rehearsing, Sire,
I fall to abject knees and beg Your grace.

KING LEWIS XVI

We give it thee. Is not thy duty sworn,
Saint-Priest, t' unroll reality, be't ne'er
So furious beneath thy Sovran's eyes?
Believe that royal crowns with riches fraught
Are symbols more of pond'rous duty than,

In sooth, of rights and airy honour. None
So well as king in harness long this knows.

Count de Saint-Priest

Thus, having sketched these sober facts and sad,
Both I and other urge Your Majesty
Forthwith to take adieu of us and all
Endang'ring here. Yourself, the Queen, as well
The children royal, will in Rambouillet
Or Rouen find a towardly resort
Where profitably You may wear the Crown.

King Lewis XVI

My Lord, here lurks what looms the bug of kings:
The secret, sly usurper. Orleans,
We say, still comfortably couches him,
High grassed, his rooted ears aswivel for
Occasions. From this seat We scarce may glide.

Marquis de la Tour Du Pin

But Sire, if You remain, it bids too fair
That hungry Lafayette commanding his
Unpleasant many and that all that rout
Of termagants who speak such passions as
Have scathed the air and ears of Paris will
But stay and shackle You, enisle You from
The Nation, set You childish lessons like
A scolding schooldame, mayhap use the Queen
And th' royal children hardly, God forfend.

Prince de Beauveau

The Revolution, repent once, will stand
Ere long the world astride. We own no time
For pendulous deliberations; let
Us riddle thought with action. Lest those men
Without attempt Your Majesty to mart
To knaves more base than they themselves, repair,
My King, I pray—and now—to regions whence
To reign as fits the royal House of France.

Necker

Your Majesty spake words more wise than these.
We must display a battled front to thieves
Would spoil the Crown and France. To haste away
May look an abdication, ticement sure
That would but set and sharp their appetite
To rule. I beg to speak My Lord the Prince
A thought impetuous. We must remain.

Prince de Beauveau

What front have we beyond the Palace Guard
At starched alert within? Our Swiss, we know,
Have ever loved His Majesty and man
Themselves with mettle and a loyalty
As fast as granite-rooted alp. They make,
Howe'er, a pimping force, if game, before
The regiment that threats the golden grille
Put to this morn. Those jades and beldams that
Have dared to visit them upon the King
And Queen show like a minatory cloud
Of humming flies come madding after blood.

A pawky wile of words on broadsheets thrown
Has rendered them inebriate with vain
Imagining, who at a drunken thought
Rose up and reeled abroad to find Versailles.
    There's nothing here to purpose, man, that may
Engage for just that independence of
The Crown so requisite to ordered rule
And, mind we ever, for the safety of
The persons royal, sacred unto France.
But little hence the monstrous swallow yawns,
Whose name is Revolution. Come You, Sire,
About and sweep serene away to height
And haven, fulcrum for a counterstroke!

NECKER

Pray, shall I take thee for a droll or shall
I trow thee earnest in this argument?
Sometimes within the leavy wood of minds
There strike the eye those leafless rampikes, dead
Though standing. Time has here conveyed me to
The sight of such a thoughtless relic. With
His Majesty hence-fleeing out o' door,
The dewy lawns and shav'n His hasting pumps
Impressing, enters nimbly at the gate,
Swung round and stonied, Orleans, brisk king
Of cockades thrice imbrued, of helpless France
Sole master, mountebank of snick'ring Hell!
    Your Majesty, I think and dare suggest
That Lafayette is scarce so minded ill
That he would check You quite or lumber You
With pressing stipulations, nay, nor would
He evilly make You o'er to fervid fools

And frigid villains. It must ill bestead
His varnished name to do aught other than
Show deference to His Christian Majesty.

Marquis de la Tour Du Pin

Do tell then, sir, in what-wise delicate
Will noble Lafayette see fit his King
To cramp and cross? What may His Majesty
Remaining here enthroned be pleased to dread?
What need for such a miscreant to cast
A king to knaves? Himself is knave enough
To nullify the steady work of time.
His heart gives not to France historical,
Of soil and peasant, King and holy Church.
In Lafayette repose the airy dreams
Of one who flies responsibility,
Who would, if only kings and priests were now
No more, unchain the France (say rather French)
Of his imagining, men good of kind—
Abstractions—nothing more. How like is *he*
To garter th' age-wove honour of the realm,
Long loomed in Christ since Clovis bare the Crown?

King Lewis XVI

Let jarring, gentles, have an end; ye do
Forget yourselves. We tell you of a truth,
We must remain, enduring what shall come.
For Providence has pinched Our compass more
Acute, We must describe a smaller arc
Of action; Orleans, the flow'ring bane

Of France—that weed would choke her blooms of
gold—
    We must uproot. Men suasible to lies
    Are always many, unto whom he sings
    Sirenic strains to flatter vanities.
    With Lafayette We shall contend, my Lords,
    As fits the wanton weather of events.
    We will ascend to quiet. Give you rest.

[*Exit the King to the right; exeunt the others to the left.*]

Scene 2

[*Into a room of the King's private apartments on the same
morning, enter the King, Who goes to a window and stares out.
Presently through a secret door enter the Queen, distraught.*]

QUEEN MARY ANTOINETTE

    Oh, blood and terror! Fiends red fanged crowd close
    Upon me! Howling savages beat flat
    The gates and bars of builded decency!
    Oh, in thy mantle shroud me, Mother mine!

KING LEWIS XVI

    Dear heart of mine, thou'rt here and harmless, safe
    With me. Thou quiverest like a netted thrush.
    Be not distract. Serene thy mind, O crowned
    Of France, and give me all the count of this.

Queen Mary Antoinette

Astir but minutes since within my rooms,
The works of day abroach—the door yet made
Upon the world without—I heard go up
A cry more mad than bedlam midst a plague.
Whereat I chanced to cast a downward sight
And spied upon the parquetry a pool
Of blood to me-wards creeping from beneath
That door made close. The guards are killed, thought I.
Now fell against the door a splitting axe,
Its bloody beak presenting hideous through
The shattered wood, its wielder speaking me
Abhorrent names. I sicked and darted for
The secret passage leading me to thee,
My panic care to go and gain from them
Would surely kill and carve me for the pikes.
Be God and Blessed Mary ever thanked
The children with the nurses stay this hour!
Oh, Lewis, they must here be swift conveyed!

King Lewis XVI

[*Addressing a guard.*]
Bring here the children royal prompt and straight.

[*Exit the guard.*]

[*Addressing the Queen.*]
That Frenchmen should be fiends! My heart for thee
Is sorrow-sick. Now weep these horrors all
Away. Upon their necks may justice do
Its direst execution! Madness gripes

Their throats, impesting heated head and breast
With hate unfathomable. Barratry,
Then brigandage is all the chronicle
Since I those curst Estates convened. The blade
Of vengeance fall and fall till murderers
Be full requited! Pray, my headlong words
Forgive; the scorpion of shame holds high
Its javelin, driving it within this heart.

Queen Mary Antoinette

In thee, decision, madbrain it though it were,
I should forgive and gladly. What shall we
Adventure, with our enemies at hand?
Oh, let us set our peckish minds to meat!

King Lewis XVI

Whate'er we do, dear wife, it scarce may be
Adventure. Deeds whipped on tantivy must
Come swift a cropper. I am vised. A way
To reign may once be found, not now. They'll have
Us to the city ere the day be done.
Please God, in Paris we shall find both bar
And purchase that may serve in prising of
That door made fast upon ourselves this day.

Queen Mary Antoinette

W'are king and queen of little worth, what more
Than carven pieces on a chequer? Near
By hours stand idle regiments by thee
Arrayed to keep the monarchy and France
From dissolution; yet thou thought'st it good—

How may I here forbear?—to set astride
The steed of high command that Besenval,
In whom thou hast a coward to the life.
For I have told of wedded years with thee,
My Lord, a score less one, should I not give
For granted how thy constant-welling doubts
Will ever work to wheedle thy resolve
Away? By sev'ral strokes of State these months
Thou chiseleds't forth a marble mind that must
As on a pedestal confess thee for
A *type* of dith'ring whilst there totter worlds
Beset of men that in the deserts of
Their wizen hearts and stiff do entertain
Of scruples none at thought of throwing down
And perishing within those worlds all things
That head and heart have made, all uses time
Therein has hallowed thorough centuries.
Hast not thyself averred how unto men
As these is France—the sum of all she was—
But pelf or, worse, *delenda* to be strown
Like Carthage, jackals left to plunder her?

King Lewis XVI

Be thou assured, the Baron Besenval
Obeys the charge I pleased to put upon
Him. Cry who would that I should now reach thwart
My heart and draw the polished streak of steel,
I will not war upon my countrymen.

Queen Mary Antoinette

Are criminals, so they be countrymen,
To mouth and smack the royal sufferance?
In trying, in thy way, to take all men
To mercy, saint with scapegrace jumbling, thou
Art unto all denying justice, yea
And mercy too. 'Tis mercy to be just.
And shall a king of France reluct to sit
Beneath the shading oak and deem as fits
A son of sainted Lewis? Be thou King
And make thy cure the punishment of foul
Hyaenas brinded o'er with crimes! Not sole
My Lord, are gallows those malefic roughs
That e'vn now tried this frame to shatter. All
Those vatic levellers, the silken lords
That take no shame, the brazen tongues on hire,
Thou should'st—though they be wont to wriggle—gaff
And weigh lest justice drop th' impartial scale
And, bursting on the angry wing, leave France
To chaos. Rule and once more breathe a king!
    Ere thee, were not the kings of France when faced
With enemies, as th' heedless shoulders of
The main, indifferent to the ocean swells
At foaming rage against them? More, did not
They hasard e'en the spilth of blameless blood
So they should cause fair Halcyon to light
Once more upon the troubled wave of France?
Pray, show a childing mind; and thou may'st yet . . .

King Lewis XVI

I thought it safe to think my fathers too

Were mortal. List, when all the Notables
Had gathered here upon the herald's cry
To help the fisc of France or ere th' Estates
We needs must call, these less than worthies soon
Discovered to the world such reticence
As plain confessed them griping of their gold,
No bowels for the peasantry reserved,
Who, disregarded, bent and staggered still
Beneath an e'er more pond'rous load of tax.
When gently called to noblemindedness,
They only mowed like monkeys dressed and hid
The coin they clutched beneath their cornered hats.
Wherefore, though they had made a leg till seam
Should split, prefer petitions till bright ink
Should be no more, more deaf to them I vowed
To prove than adder fore the charmer's drone.
    I ventured hope how when the three Estates
Were met they might burst out the stopple all
The Notables had hammered home. The Third,
Howe'er, betraying canine appetite,
Grew big with taking down the other twain.
This couched impond'rable it is that waits
At Paris. May not something yet be hoped
Of that assembly? Pliable they're not,
But mulcible by my concessions they
May prove. I wonder not how they might have
Me the anointed plowman of that vast
Emprise whereto they turn the calloused hand.
Indeed, in many yet may reason reign.

QUEEN MARY ANTOINETTE

Does it require to be grotesque? That warm

Employment thy discrowning and the death
Of Catholic France embraces. One may like
Thee to the fabled Pythoness of eld,
Who, perched upon the three-legg'd throne, inhaled
Such vapours from the breathing vents beneath
As turned her reason. Scarce her ravings more
Incomprehensible could sound than thine.

    As trenchant policy, appeasement's sole
Within the gift of magnanimity.
A conqueror, an iron rod in grip,
May think no scorn to reach concession down
To foes by him subdued, who thus to him
May give devotion felt and grateful both.

    And when in time of mind were coddled heads
To sacrifice propense? Thy speeches to
The Notables could speak no meaning in
Their pearly ears and spoilt, mere lapdogs most
Long cosseted of kings, emasculate
With empty honours, unto whom there glimpse
In sight more riches now than they had dreamed
The day of their foregathering to thee.
Before their saucer eyes there lie the fields
Of France's treasures, lands of Church and King.
Howe'er, the factions, not the Fronde, are e'vn
Th' infesting bot that burrows 'neath the hide
Of France to work her ruin, thine as well.

[*A clamour of many voices begins to be heard from without the open windows.*]

King Lewis XVI

Now what shall noise upon this morning air

To drown the lamentations of the spoiled
And tongueless bird? The public voice, I think.

Queen Mary Antoinette

Its cries fetch terror from my tripping heart.
Oh, Lewis, canst thou try out what they say?

King Lewis XVI

They cry, methinks, for bread less dear. In fine,
They're fain to roar us back to Paris. From
This morn 'tis tumult and combustion, for
They've driven us at last to ground and now
Will have their worry; 'pon this back they'll do
An unremitting execution. Know
I say in figure; thou'lt be safe. The pledge
Of France (thy spouse anent thee) clips thee round.

[*He embraces Her and begins to walk to a window. Enter the Marquis de la Tour du Pin escorting the Dauphin and the Dauphine.*]

Good morrow, ducklings; let me fold you to
This harried heart. To Mother hence you now.
La Tour du Pin, I bid thee welcome. We
Would be apprised of these Our visitors.

Marquis de la Tour Du Pin

I come with hope to see You well. An't please
You, Sire, I think 'twere wise to disappoint
Th' wide window's lure to look abroad their veils.

King Lewis XVI

Go hence and, drawing back the lace, describe.

[*La Tour du Pin walks to a window.*]

Marquis de la Tour Du Pin

I own no shock to spy below the mob.
Both bloods and dowsabelles, and wizan corks
Of ev'ry shape, upraise the greasy chin,
Their ruddy faces frankly speaking much
Inebriation. They would see You, Sire;
But more, I fear, they would the Queen behold.

The Mob

The King! The Queen! We'll have Them forth! Come out!
The Queen! The Queen! We'll have the Queen!

[*A single voice is heard.*]
                                        Step forth
The window, Ma'am, we'd pay respects. Ha ha!

[*Another voice.*]
We'll see Her writhe and throw Her jeweled rind
'Afore us!

[*A third voice.*]
                Bread, or to the gallows straight!

Marquis de la Tour Du Pin

A murrain meet these cattle! Sire, there needs
A regiment to clear the Marble Court.
It wakes the blood to hear such treason tongued.

King Lewis XVI

'Tis sole a captain cold in disaccord
With kings may waft a poor maroon as dry,
My Lord, as biscuit o'er these swollen seas
Of discontent. That man is Lafayette,

[*Enter the Prince de Beauveau, who whispers in the
King's ear.*]

Who comes.

[*Enter the Marquis de Lafayette.*]

         Lord Lafayette, We had not thought
Thou would'st this morn have graced this chamber of
Our presence. Art thou come a captain to
Thy King? This clay of royalty and His
Have need; the House of France is set upon
This day. Wherefore, the eyes of ages roll
Upon thee, searching close the man they hold.

Marquis de Lafayette

Your Majesty, I come—this know—to see
Your person safe to Paris; quite in care
I have Your safety, Sire, not less the Queen's
And royal children's. Pledge of this upon

This sword I swear as son of all the French.
Here forth, Your ward in constant watch I'll bear.

King Lewis XVI

We scarce expected other, careful sir.
The congress yond the windows makes to cry
The Queen and Us without; pray hold Us bound
To speak with Her upon the marrow of
This matter holloed high this instant morn.

[Leaving Lafayette, the King approaches the Queen.]

It sorrows me to say, sweet Queen, whose reign
Is [*pointing to His heart*] here not less than there, how
duty bids
Us go upon the balcony to greet
Our guests, who tumult like the wind-wrought deep.
The children too must bear us company.
Strike all that emblems fear, for should'st thou there
Run up the smallest banderol that reads
The mott "*Hic regnat timor*" and thou shalt
But set an edge more keen to appetites
E'vn now sharp-set in cold ferocity.

Queen Mary Antoinette

I feel the panic mouse that darts now here
Now there t' evade the falcon's closing fist.
But know me natheless for the Queen of France.
Though heart beat high, though I should yet weep down
The sun, with thee I'll go compliable
To God, so grant He strength to me, as thee.

[Exeunt the King, the Queen, and the royal children to the balcony, where they can be seen by the audience.]

THE MOB

[Above an uproarious din, a single voice is heard.]
Now, throw your eyes at that!

[Another voice is heard.]
                                        Her Majesty
Shows weaker than a pot o' strike-me-dead!

[Raucous laughter from many.]

[A third single voice is heard.]
We'll feed upon Their homage, and we'll have
Their prompt obedience or chine Them at
The neck and drink at once Their smoking blood!

[Several voices and then all are heard.]
To Paris They! To Paris They! Hurrah!
To Paris! To Paris! To Paris! To Paris! To Paris!
To Paris! To Paris! To Paris! To Paris! To Paris!

[A curtain is drawn on the scene.]

Scene 3

[*In the afternoon of the same day, in the Marble Court of the Palace of Versailles, enter from the right the King, the Queen, the royal children, the Prince de Beauveau, the Marquis de la Tour du Pin, others of the King's retinue, and members of the Swiss Guard. From the left, enter the Marquis de Lafayette, members of the revolutionary soldiery, and the mob. At the centre, a large coach with an open door is present. Some of the revolutionary soldiers bear flintlocks with bayonets, on some of which are impaled loaves of bread, on others the severed heads of the murdered Swiss Guards.*]

MARQUIS DE LAFAYETTE

Your Majesties, the ceremonials
Of polished words aside, grasp this: within
This coach You go from here bastilled—enisled
From power absolute. My deeds, be sure,
Do but dispatch the People's will, from whom
All true dominion emanates from now.

KING LEWIS XVI

Nor thou nor they, my Lord, might bear or wield
Authority except by God 'twere giv'n.
This head anoint forth phial from Heaven winged
Was by the Christ of God Himself paled round
With crusted orbs and crosses, unto Whom
We shall not long from this give trepid count
Of Our poor scepter's ev'ry nod and sweep.

Marquis de Lafayette

Such Gothic sentiments so quaintly said
Bespeak a pretty superstition that
Will vanish like the dew beneath the sun
And sober rule of reason rational.
Use understood and dateless—hallowed of
A doltish herd—must like a needless crutch
Be thrown forever down. 'Tis Liberty
To feel and think and do as reason shall
Illume the rising road and shadowed, Sire.

King Lewis XVI

Thine intellection oft becomes a bright
But arid eye that wilts and withers flow'r
And fruit of high imagination; worse,
My Lord, it resolutely stares from 'twixt
Two nubilous blinkers that should ward away
All scotch and spoor of cause and purpose. Have
Thy reason, though unreasonable, but know
It for the flat soup-maigre it will prove,
Of which its only meat is matter gross,
Its single, straightened ground of knowledge clutched
And secretly desired as giving on
A fineless, dark abysm found to full
With do-as-ye-shall-please confess thee ne'er
So furious to hear it worded out.
    Moreover, We much think, my learned Lord,
Thy reason's realm is not the dome of sky;
It homes within the mind of everyman.
Now, after day meets dusk that candle's flame
Of one man's wav'ring wit will scarcely serve

To show the way beyond his humid nose.
That custom thou contemn'st is e'en that torch
That daubed about with th' concentrated pitch
Of immemorial experience
Will lend its lambent beams to lead aright.
This said, no lamp, 'tis sure, may lead so well
As grace irradiant from Heaven high.
At end, naught else but this will ever do.

QUEEN MARY ANTOINETTE

Your Majesty, against Your tiring ere
To Paris We shall hence be pulled away,
Pray cool and sleek the heart and recollect
The hard-breathed mind.
[*Addressing Lafayette.*]
       Retire, sir; grant Us leave
To enter here with quiet port and mien.

[*Lafayette withdraws.*]

[*Addressing the King.*]
I durst not longer idle, Lewis, long
This perilous ventilation. Ev'ry word
Thou wovest made thee royal more, but whilst
Thou loomed'st, thy listener's flash of eye bewrayed
Him waxing inly wroth. Unwise, thought I,
To breed ill blood in this cockaded bane,
Who yet may fail to hold us fast from hurt.

King Lewis XVI

I own how I perceived him less than pleased.
Th' rough rasp of harsh events, as well I see,
Has sharped thy wits more keen than ere they proved.

Queen Mary Antoinette

From such as he fired words are ne'er to fear,
But retribution cold and waiting in
The way. To candid treason he will soon
Abandon him; from now he'll shadow bleak
Upon the land. The wheelèd shroud awaits.

[*The King and the Queen proceed to enter the coach, the
royal children being already within it.*]

The Mob

[*Amidst a general tumult, a voice is heard.*]
We'll swaddle such as this in tender bands
Until we make of monarchs mummies. Cast
About Him cords, ye beggars; frap them tight!

[*A crone astride a cannon in the van speaks.*]
There's none for them to fear; we'll roister fore
'Em like the merry dolphins! Flowing tides
Of tipple are to draw. To Paris swim
And all be well!
[*Addressing an impaled head and proffering a mug.*]
                    Drink, dearie. How thy gob's
Agape for what may wet the dusty tongue!

King Lewis XVI

[Addressing the Queen.]
Their shouts become a shoot of arrows swift
To find this labouring heart. Upon this brow
Are visited this day the piercing sins
Of kings before me gone. With theirs mine own
Are tightly raddled round; so sharp are they,
Their points do disappear to daunted sight.
Be expiation, Lord, their sinking in.

*[The King and the Queen enter the coach, which presently
rolls away preceded and followed by everyone else, the Swiss
Lifeguards marching in close array about it.]*

ACT 5

Scene 1

[*At the Palace of the Tuileries, enter the King, Who walks to a desk and sits at it to work; presently, enter a valet, who saunters to the desk and impudently leans over the King's shoulder idly to peer at the papers He is reading.*]

KING LEWIS XVI

Now, get thee hence, thou stinking ape in braid
And buttons! Never nigh Us creep again!

[*Exit the valet sauntering.*]

[*Enter the Queen.*]

Is Paris not a narrow prison, wife,
The valets round us very jailers? In
Duress we dwell uncharged and unaccused;
And feeble as a fly, I beat against
The meshes weaving fine about us. Truth,
My spirits, drooping since the Notables,
Now sound the black abysm of despond;
No man than I more tried his country to
Improve; no man more throughly failed. At shut
Of day a swart familiar comes to stage
Before my inward eye a masque of drear

Remembrance—pageants of defeat. "A game
Is here," they urge of th' agitable prize
For pow'r, "that's little worth the candle. Come
Away and court serene forgetfulness
Of pain." And there an end. But soon I see
The Christ fixed fast upon the Cross and will
Not follow. Duty carpenters the cross
Of kings. From heavy languishment I've striv'n
In vain, howe'er, my torpid limbs to raise;
From feath'ry couch to splint'ry cross I yet
Must go a progress. Help my hebetude,
O God and guardians of France and me!

Queen Mary Antoinette

So let us slip the chafing irons, leave
As on the velvet feet of cats far ere
This beadledom shall hear the crow of dawn.
Repair we straight to outlands where midst friends
We may our jaded eyes cast high to see
Our billowing troubles furling swift away.

King Lewis XVI

Thou limn'st and blushest out a canvas fair
To contemplate, my sweeting. Oh, to speak
An honest man, to be away from all
The jacks-in-office thronging here, who jar
Like th' angry clam of sour-sounding bells!
In act a king noway am I; howe'er,
Well yond the suffocating toils of this
Captivity there waits what good Beauveau
So fitly nempt the fulcrum whence to move

The mountain of misgovernment here wreathed
Like mythic gods in metaphysic cloud.
    Ne, not beyond the pale of France we'll fly,
But only to a towery fastness in
The farther provinces. Though rolling much
In peril 'cross the swells and vales of France—
As on the undulating brim of an
Abyss—with help of Heaven we shall raise
The walls and tow'rs of Montmédy, where, far
From Paris, leverage we shall have wherewith
To prize and crack the Constitution, sore
In need of all revision as may make
It unexceptionable to God. Within
My conscience, guilt wox great when, yielding ground
That had with martyrs' blood been long ago
Aspersed, I dared to put my shame-rid name
To that so foul decree that forthwith bade
All priests unsay their fealty to Rome.
    Upon a night forecast with care our deed
Of flight shall be ado. Thy friend of years,
Good Fersen, would be much of service in
The blessed execution of this plan,
Who must prevent its being anything
In murmur. Lafayette has everywhere
His swiveling ears—in slum and salon cocked
Alike. The day we took of sweet Versailles
Our sad adieu, I wondered how, in sooth,
He could restrain himself from visiting
Our baggage. Ah, thou prov'st a physic fit
To breathe a turgid vein of one so flown
With melancholia as I have been!

[*Enter Madame Elizabeth, sister to the King.*]

Elizabeth, we've plans afoot to haste
Away from here by night; thou'lt come with us.

QUEEN MARY ANTOINETTE

I must premonish still, my Lord. I stand
An evidence to God and testify
How constitutions ne'er consent with kings.
Thou'dst err again if thou should'st sully thine
Anointed hand by striking in with rank
Republicans. The hand by thee so struck
Would enter thee, I fear, and thou must reign
In craven wise of English puppet kings.
    Within the mad and multiloquious
Assembly summoned by the vaunted vote,
The right and left, to wit the Girondins
And Jacobins, are but the bended set
Of teeth upon the Revolution's saw
(Pulled gaily to and fro by devils loosed
From Hell.) Some bended left, some bended right,
They'll natheless jointly fell the ancient tree
Of France and rip it all to lumber. Would'st
Thou, Lewis, willingly preside o'er this?

KING LEWIS XVI

So prosper this my plan, I shall be clothed
With pow'rs executive to do whatso
May damp or temper the Assembled should
They froward prove. The public man need not
Be sole a king, fair wish. Indeed, I own

An admiration long-awak'ning for
The English polity. Let come reform
Polite and gradual, the Monarchy
Preserved as that yonside the flying Sleeve
Of Ocean set by God between the twain,
Forever France, forever England, pight
For emulation long this vale and time.

QUEEN MARY ANTOINETTE

Oh, Lewis, wilt thou ne'er tuition take?
Oh, must thou never know the posture of
The world? A king must e'er try truth from cant.
Elizabeth, thou art his sister, soul
As well of counter-revolution, speak
Him of his yonder cousinage in crowns.

MADAME ELIZABETH

The English kings have seen their powers fleet
Since Henry severed Canterbury from Rome;
For th' English aristocracy, waxed proud
And pursy on their spoil of Holy Church,
O'erbare their poorer sovran, whom they haled
From bridge, where once he steered, to prow, whence, stiff
And armless, he but stares the hissing seas.
Th' assembled here will ape their Parliament,
One thing except: they'll urge democracy.

    Dear brother, all my care's to succour thee,
To see thee King and true. Because thou own'st,
As one should say, this flow'r-sprent realm of France,
The garden of this royal house fixed firm
And rooted deep by mystic Charlemagne,

'Tis in thy fundamental cure as King
To hand this country strong and thriven to
Thy son and heir. The demagogues would be
Ephem'ral hirelings dowered for a day
With th' usufruct of France, who, for they own
Not this demesne, nor can, and therefore in
Her hard-won assets have no stake, must be
Much like to grope through ev'ry prosperous purse
And pocket with abandon, reaching out
Such coin as may be crowded into those
More wizen purses at the waists of men
Whose votes have bought such spoliation plain,
Not less made sleek these ministrants in pow'r.

    As flatterers in blood, they'll soothe their daws
With comfortable words, so chos'n as not
To harsh them aught with stringent calls and cold
To assiduity or thrift. In fine,
Prosperity will wane, and poverty
Will wax as industry and enterprise
Lose all once-wonted charms. What man, prone or
To diligence or indolence, would work
When on the drones are show'red the gathers reaped
(Or ripped) from all the simpletons that toil?

    What then the issue of this polity
If not a disincentive to produce
And much incentive to become, or late
Or soon, a lumpish pensioner of the State?
This stealage justice men will dare to style.

    Now, throwing o'er the sceptre royal, men seize
The pestle of democracy to mill
The family until it be a dust
Of sundered individuals that may

Be roused and huffed whence'er the wind of whim
Is setting—naked fore the stone-eyed state,
As fore the scribbling rabble of the hour.
In ev'ry realm, dependency upon
The democratic state will smother all
The mutual dependence lambent now
Within the family hearth. Democracy
Is death, an enemy just yond that door.

King Lewis XVI

Enough to say I have a sibyl for
A sister. From thy beaten breast come aye
The deep-drawn sigh, as from thy cracking throat
The wailing threne. My heart yet gives to me
How France is served by moderation. Harsh
Thy words and sharp; thou woundest to the blood.
I ween, good sister, thou hast drawn the long
Bow near to shatters and vermilioned all
This tale, creating travesty of truth.
Thou word'st as thou wert tranced or stitched as tight
As button unto whims without a seam
With th' present tissue of reality.

Madame Elizabeth

I've limned for thee this ev'n the essence and
The issue of a monstrous lie, not more,
The tide of which is making as we speak.

King Lewis XVI

Good ladies, silence forth; unkennel no
More baying notions from your minds. From this

To Montmédy, nor any cavilling more.

Queen Mary Antoinette

Before Your sovran will have I not dropped
A curtsey ever?

[*Exeunt the King and the Queen.*]

Madame Elizabeth

Give you ready sleep.

[*Exit Madame Elizabeth.*]

Scene 2

[*An early June evening in a deserted street of Varennes. A
large carriage stands to one side. Enter the King, followed by
the Queen, the two royal children, Madame Elizabeth, and
the Count Axel von Fersen. Enter from another direction a
coachman.*]

Coachman

We daren't further whip these horses up,
Which ev'n from Paris to this dorp have dashed
And hurtled as by madded hornets swarmed.
But one league more, my Lord, and you shall grieve
To see them sudden down and dead as stones.
Before the lash we dare lay smartly to
And play again the supple reins, we must
Here hitch a new and spanking team that may

From hence respond to crack and gee and haw
Or we must wait the whips and gees of them
That miles behind us have us hard in chase.

COUNT VON FERSEN

But, man, that side this bridge a troop of horse
Awaits that, ere the wearied sun shall this
Day totter down the westward sky, will have
Us safe from this Varennes to Montmédy.

KING LEWIS XVI

What says our man, good Fersen? Are the lamps
Of Montmédy to glimmer in our eyes
This gloom of ev'n? Like shrouding birds that drive
Full swift before the storm, we long for sleep
Innested safe 'neath hospitable spires.

COUNT VON FERSEN

He now assevered that except we find
Cooled hackneys to replace our jaded team,
Those spires are little like to rise and take
Us in—are like, my Liege, to stay beneath
That utmost brink and blue of tired sight.

KING LEWIS XVI

[*Somewhat abstracted.*]
There's One that rose far since and even now
Will take us in do we but ask in hope.
[*Recovering His demeanour.*]
Yet farther must we cast behind us those
From Paris sweating after us these hours,

Against they overtake us—fang and glut
Us down once more to cramp and sad duress.
More swift than silver-quick, dear friends, go hence
And throw your eyes about these silent streets
For stablemen with roadsters that may pull
Us headlong o'er those yonder spans. Thence, with
The lances waiting us, we'll fly as straight
As feathered dart to smiling Montmédy.

[*Exeunt running Count von Fersen and the coachman.
The King and the Queen dash severally and frantically from
house to house, knocking on the doors. No one answers, until at
one house the King knocks and the door opens revealing a sol-
dier bearing a musket and closely facing Him. The King starts
back in horror. Enter M. Drouet, a postmaster, who, having
earlier recognized the King, has been pursuing the royal carriage for some while. He approaches the King from behind.
During the following exchanges, a crowd of townspeople and
soldiers slowly gathers.*]

Drouet

His Majesty is welcome. Grieved I am
To see Him touched i' the wind this pretty ev'n,
His brow much giving dew, His gentle Queen
As one by heedless barber blooded white.

King Lewis XVI

And which, pray tell, of Our good subjects, liege
And loyal, speaks this dwindling day with such
Address his care for's sovran King and's Queen?

DROUET

Drouet, Your Majesty, till this fair strait
The Posting-Master at Sainte-Menehould,
The People's jack-e'er-at-a-pinch. Miles since,
I joyed to spy both Your exalted self
And Your espousèd Queen in car ensconced.
I could but toast this starry smile as with
A stirrup cup and give You chase.

                                 I've thought,
And long, them omened ill, the ways that put
More miles twixt men and Paris—pitted roads,
My Liege, of doubtful wheeling—think You not?

KING LEWIS XVI

We think thou stand'st a scarlet rogue before
Us. Crowned and duly chrismed father of
This firstborn realm of Christendom, about
The good of all her children We now go,
Who hinders which is gallows. Have a care;
Let not the bounden doings of thy King.

DROUET

The French account themselves a comity
Of bonded brothers, Sire, cast firm upon
Their freedom. Ev'ryhow and ev'rywhen
The trow'l I ply as paviour for their way
And whim. In Paris they will have You now.
   Alas, the children royal make a lip
And sob; they long their sanded eyes to close.

[*The Count von Fersen approaches and addresses Drouet.*]

Count von Fersen

How dar'st thou take thy betters short, thou worm!
Stand not thou drolling with His Majesty,
Thou vacant of decorum and respect.
Thy miserable words are spinach. By
Thy matted head and mealy beard, thou'lt hold
The same and soon, thou pimping rat, for trim
Twixt hoodman's blade and block. Now slither hence!

Drouet

Pray, think no more of *straying* hence. Nor thou
Nor they shall ever stand that side the bridge
T''inspire the far-blown, spacious airs of France;
I give you one shall unto Paris have
You all ere day shall on the morrow set.

[*M. Drouet withdraws somewhat. Enter M. Romeuf, Aide-de-Camp to the Marquis de Lafayette, and the Mayor of Varennes, M. Sauce, along with several members of the National Guard. From this point the light gradually fades.*]

Romeuf

Your Majesty, I have the honour to
Convey to You as to Her Majesty
The Queen, the greetings and the heart's regard
Of both the National Assembly and
My Lord Commander, General Lafayette.

King Lewis XVI

The seeming of thy words and visage speak
As thou wert feal to thy King. It masks

A calculus of cold rebellion, need
We say, Sir Sprent-With-Dew? The pith these ears
Will have. Troll out the burden of this verse.

ROMEUF

Your Majesty, I am instructed by
Their honours and am here dispatched to You
Ev'n by my Lord, the Marquis, to express
Their wish how You and all here present should
Return forthwith to Paris, where th' events
Of these untoward hours may be addressed.

QUEEN MARY ANTOINETTE

The sooner said the sooner wept. Oh, will
There never be from bitterness reprieve?
The nemesis of kings is Lafayette!
Himself he streams the evil ensign of
The Revolution, th' end of which is France
Disintegrate in blood and chaos. Faults
We own—Our vanities of youth; but now
We put as softly to the breast the good
Of France as erst We put Our suckling babes.
Our coming hence was not to safe ourselves,
But sole to wrest this realm from them would sap
And spill this firstborn daughter of the Church.

ROMEUF

I stand abashed and desolate before
Her Majesty; my solemn plight stands thwart
My heart and hand, which latter palsied thus
It may not now draw steel and foin it with

The enemies environing You here.

Madame Elizabeth

With words that delicately glance at teen
And terrors still to be, thou look'st, withal,
As one that might be gentled of a tap
Upon the gilded shoulder. Know, young man,
Thou wait'st upon a devil—speak'st as one
Upon an embassade from Hell. Thou know'st
It not at this, meseems, but shalt, and soon.
The wheat by rot and rust is oft surprised.

[*M. Romeuf bows while stepping back several paces.
M. Sauce and the members of the National Guard also
move back.*]

King Lewis XVI

There's nothing for't. The trees shade long and hope,
As well as day, lies dying. Morn, new sprung
From ashen night, will see us fetched again
Like felons back to sad Dystopia.
Now kings go scorned and gyved; now realms disedge
Of demagogues the wolvish appetite.
Pulled down from my once honour, I look up
To see my power fleet. We hither came
Like sea-beat oarsmen pulling frantic through
The rushing cliffs. They crush us now, our foe
And all my headlong fondness met, ourselves
Between and bleeding. Know, by ev'ry man
From now I am forbid and spat upon.
My reign is yaw and shipping angry seas.

In fine, I am become unable. God
His grace provide. We cannot more than pray.

Queen Mary Antoinette

The darkful time for showing glint of tears
Is this. Upon the dreaded bright of dawn
Will come from gath'ring throats to frighted ear
Th' inevitable crake of terror. Now
Each shadow round us deep'ning seems to mask
A watching presence. O sweet God, make safe
Our souls and persons! Keep us in Thy care.

Madame Elizabeth

What though our long and weary carriage back
To Paris put the mob in highest leg,
Its pandars venge our brief escape with cold
Indignities—though we be counted dusts
And things of nought—oh, let us not unbend!
Before we join the vast before us gone,
We'll quit us Christians; that, as turns this plough
Of persecution, we should drop as seeds
Of blood. Soon thence the faith may follow flush
And mantling fruit for God be many. Hard
At pray'r let us address ourselves against
The morrow miseries. Blood-ripe we're culled.

King Lewis XVI

Dear blood mine own, speak not as thou should'st needs
Be spilled upon this furrowed France, for thou,
As well the Queen and these sweet cossets, shalt
Go quite secure. The shroud of night is cast;

We must to bed. To all give dreamless sleep.

[*The King nods to M. Romeuf, signaling that He and those who fled with Him are ready to be escorted away. Exeunt omnes.*]

Scene 3

[*In Paris, near a bridge on the Seine, enter from the left George James Danton; enter from the right Peter Lewis Roederer, Syndic of the Department of Paris. It is August 10, 1792. The tocsin is sounding.*]

DANTON

Pray, Roederer, how do the Royals in
That monumental cage in shot of this?

ROEDERER

Was't thou, Danton, invoked this madding din
That ere the soundless dawn had beamed through blind
And curtain drawn was full at roar within
This Afric heat? This morn all Paris has
The staggers; King to scabby scroyl, all hearts
Are beating birds.
           The King and His do on
Dejection, sir,—each day a deeper hue.

DANTON

The judgement of the People is at hand.
The Revolution full in spectacle

Thou'lt see from now. No man of us without
His part to play. For thee, 'tis trace the steps
That brought thee here and coax that foolish King
And's riggish wife to leave the Tuileries
And shelter with th' Assembly, whence He might
Be dextrously put once and finally down.

ROEDERER

No wish have I to pick once more a path
Through braves would kill a man that looks them squint.
They burn like stinking brimstones spat from Hell.

DANTON

[*Taking him by the throat.*]
Then look them not asquint, thou bleating shirk!
Go not thou on the instant to the King,
And by this throat's lace, when I shall have done
With thee, thou'lt name him blest that yonder runs
Against a raving anthropophagus.

ROEDERER

I live to serve the Revolution, sir.
Thou know'st than I there breathes no man more burns
To lend upon its service very bleeds
Of sweat. Cry out upon the tyranny!

DANTON

Thy time to bleed is come. Now lest thy wife
Untimely widow, to the Tuileries
Make feet and use the sleights of suasion on
The King, rememb'ring Him of perils to

His kin, not least to the Apparent. Play
The wagtail. Look thou smoothe Him; urging naught
Against the hair. Upon His yielding, wait
Him to th' Assembly as to lord thou wert
The constant man. In few, ere cockshut get
Him gone. I shall require of thee, be sure,
A render of this do. Thou'rt watched; across
The day thou creep'st beneath thy multiple
Reflection in the many-trellised eyes
Of aphides at suck, who whisper to
The hornet Revolution late and soon.

ROEDERER

Do stoutly on, my heart, thy plate of steel;
Resolve and man thyself with th' inward axe
Of bowelless execution. I am gone.

[*Exit.*]

DANTON

The heated blood soon cooled and clung. Ha! Ha!
Pale ensign of the craven heart, that face.

[*Exit.*]

Scene 4

[*Into the Chamber of the Legislative Assembly, many deputies present, enter Roederer, followed in dejection by the King, the Queen, the royal children, and Madame Elizabeth. Some in the Chamber rise. Fusillades and truculent cries of the mob without are audible. Among the deputies present in the Chamber are John Francis Honoré Merlet, President of the Assembly, and Francis Chabot, a deputy sitting far to the left.*]

Roederer

Lord President, Their Majesties, arrived
With these the children royal—with Them come
Madame the sister to the King—beg leave
To shelter here from perils imminent
Without this guarded pale of governing.

Merlet

The honour of this body cannot but
Engage for ev'ry of Their Highnesses,
Ere ev'ry else, of course, Their Majesties.

King Lewis XVI

[*Addressing Madame Elizabeth.*]
Here wafts a wind reminds a man there was
A thing rejoiced i' the unembarrassed name
Of fealty. Shall we be kindly used?

Madame Elizabeth

No doubt, my Lord; and if the kind of kings
And queens is roughly used in France of late,
Why, we may feel a kindly use indeed.

King Lewis XVI

The world has worked to spoil me clean of hope.

Madame Elizabeth

Ourselves may never slip the hopples here,
But One that broke the stony jaws of death
And o'er their shattered verge rose rathe and like
The blinding, gilded morn can will us free.

King Lewis XVI

I stagger strook i' th' gasping wind, stuck deep
Within the heart. Grant God that, till I lie
A sheeted corse, I shall be constant at
The service of *my* King, Whom I but late—
Cheeks growing quick with shame—re-crucified
By lett'ring "Lewis" cross the blighted leaf
Writ o'er with impudence—wrought e'en of these
Assembled—bidding clerics ev'ry one
T' abjure his plighted ligeance unto Rome
And graft him on this sacrilegious tree
Of license. Th' eldest shoot of tendrilled Church
Was thus strown down. The world is ground to dust.

Chabot

Lord President, I beg your leave to let
What some may deem the jarring voice. Pray, how
May we, deputed of the People, speak
Thus curbed—so might we venture—*lumbered* with
The presence royal? Clear 'tis specified
Within the Constitution how debate
We may not urge in presence of the King.

A Deputy

Requires it now that from the parted lips

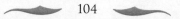

Of ev'ry minute's mushroom royal oaks
Shall take a puff of scorn? If so decrees
The Constitution, wherefore need we *now*
Debate? Are we such shabby men as pinch
The simple rites of hospitality?
The face of Liberty is here dislimned.

CHABOT

The People's enemies it is—and with
Them those compliable—that Liberty
Deface. And is that fair Celestial
Remote and smiling, goddess after whom
We ardent votaries have daily breathed,
Whose influence 'tis ours to magnify
Till all this agued earth be set alight,
To favour just that glacial crew that scout
Her? Sure, the sacred business, ev'ry the
Minutest, of the Nation must be aired,
All perils answered. Ev'ry matter else
Is straws and ciphers, as we cast accounts.

A DEPUTY

As idle words as ever tripped from tongue.
And shall, Lord President, the King's and Queen's
Insulted Majesties, as well Their blood's
Dishonoured Highnesses, come something short
Of meriting our heed, fare forthwith hence,
Reposing Their exhausted hopes within
The bosom of the gracious ones that crake
And cry without? Pray might it harsh—if but
A thought—against the agitable kibes

Of conscience—twang perchance the jangling nerve
Of Nation—t' immolate these sev'ral lives,
Th' Anointed—ev'n His flesh and lineage—
Upon the altar of efficiency?

CHABOT

Be 't wide away from us to wish upon
The House of France discomfort. Spy we not,
Lord President, a box below should serve
To segregate the Royal Family from
All weighty matters heaping high upon
Our shoulders here this legislative day?

MERLET

Yon closet standing free and pierced with grilles
To put the th' inhabitant Recorder full
Within the earreach of this Chamber's grave
And many-sounding voice has been proposed
For an expedient whereunto may yet
Their Majesties absent Them safe from our
Proceedings at this present. All attend:
Say out an Aye all ye who yield accord.

MOST OF THE DEPUTIES

Aye.

MERLET

Say out an Nay all ye who frown dissent.

A Few of the Deputies

Nay.

Merlet

The Ayes prevail. Wherefore, Their Majesties
And all Their train will now betake them to
That room and sequestration whereunto
These deputies have eloquently spoke.

Chabot

Lord President, with numbers Wisdom dwells,
'Tis sure, who fast beneath the carnival
Of teeming men assumes her whist abode.
'Tis she who upward breathes those raptures that
Have fulled and put in swoon for Liberty
These sev'ral years the hearts and heads of men,
Whose will, nay whim, so schooled of her, is ours.
  Fair Liberty, O harrower of hearts,
Abrupt our cloddish loyalties to all
Would let our love for thee, nor hearth, nor blood,
Nor land, nor priest, nor monarch. Brotherhood
Within thy constant gaze: not more our need.

[*Applause from the left of the Assembly is heard and is
promptly taken up by the remainder of the deputies. Escorted
to the Reporter's box by soldiers of the National Guard, the
King, the Queen, the royal children, and Madame Elizabeth
enter it. Enter quickly two stagehands in plain costume (e.g.,
leotards of subdued colour)—one person from the left, the other
from the right—and open the audience side of the Recorder's
box so that the audience may see and hear the action to take*

*place within it. Their duty performed, exeunt the stagehands
stage left and stage right.*]

KING LEWIS XVI

The guards that erst by doorpost cried, "The King!";
Raised forth the wide parade twixt rolling drum
And silver tongue of trumpets wild the "Vive"
Unfeigned; and as in days of Charlemagne
Strode swift before us making way have faced
About and to the present dropt the pike.

QUEEN MARY ANTOINETTE

Who here our sullen jailers are become.

KING LEWIS XVI

If sole within this little ark afloat
That brim of heaving Ocean, I shall reign
A King; all you alone, my dears, shall be
My subjects, sweeter lieges far than nymphs
And pretty lambs. One day we'll walk without
These weary walls, desporting careless on
The fallow, who, yclad in smock of weeds
And flowers, entertains the rabble birds
And all that timeless band, burnt August and
Her thousand murm'ring children.
[*Addressing the Dauphin.*]

                                    Sit by me.

MADAME ELIZABETH

O prince abused, are oaths and vows in France
But vapor? Prim hypocrisy self-nimned

With righteousness has gained this place; upon
The brow of nearly all about us she
Has perched; for, having blithely sworn away
Integrity, they scrupulously do
Their might, as must affront an honest eye,
To cleave to all may in the scribble of
The Constitution speed their purpose to
The King's humiliation—leading thence
But to the Same's defenestration. Let
Them put their spectacles on this: an if
Their vaunted Constitution bars debate
In presence of the Sovran, sure nor less
It guaranties the person of the Same
From violation; sole the reason for
Your presence here, dear Lewis, ours as well,
Within this noisome den is e'vn the fact
How Your self person has this direful day
Been violated.
             Squinnying through this grille,
I reckon how we float as worthy on
These waters as a twiggen basket. Lo
Where solemn comes an officer of Your
Most loyal Swiss, who must be yet on guard
Within the Tuileries. I think he would
Have words with You.

King Lewis XVI

            An ear, then, let Us lend.

[*Enter Captain Durler, commander of the Swiss Guards on duty at the Palace of the Tuileries. He briskly walks to the Recorder's box.*]

Captain Durler

[*Addressing Madame Elizabeth at the grille.*]
I give Your Highness greetings from the true. [*He briefly puts his hand to his heart.*]
That I had e'er been born to see my Lord,
The King, thus contumeliously used!

Madame Elizabeth

I know, good Captain, how in hearing of
The King thou'lt give not all thy sorrow words.

Captain Durler

[*He profoundly bows to the King and addresses Him.*]
I joy to see His Majesty but grieve
To see Him here thus rudely cabined. Sire,
I come to plead Your mercy, begging You
To execute a right-about and now
Unsay Your late-delivered hest that my
Command stand forthwith down and stack their smeared
And smoking arms, which even now are all
May stay the grisly fate that from the rout
Afront them stares them, not to terror, but
To iron constancy though ne'er so much
The selfsame mob have lanced at them the threat
To drink their blood ere day himself should sink
Expiring in his crimson bleed of light.

King Lewis XVI

Meseems, dear Captain, for as opposites
They stand you, thou canst only give them with

A brush o'er-freighted of the darker hues.
We cannot bear the ugsome thought that men
Of France should hack and shoot their fellows, less
That We should urge such frights of fratricide.
We venture how those men but tartly speak,
As toilers will, a moment's spleen. They know
And well that We this morning since are gone
From forth the Tuileries. They face you yet
And will not crowd away, the thing shows clear,
Since thy command, all stiff as steel, still glare
Suspicion and defiance at their lines.
Put by the sword and they will give and melt
Away as ice caressed of April air.

Captain Durler

Their curses stream like crimson ensigns of
Their rank intent to have us dead, and dead
By many times again, were't doable,
So might they slake their raging thirst for blood.
They stand a crowd of scatheful men well found
With blades and shot—and brooding, Sire, upon
A hatch of horrors. O'er our heads there wheels
Death certain and atrocious. Carry they
The stairs that rise to our position and
E'er th' evening candles gutter in their tombs
Our severed heads from rebel pikes will gape.

King Lewis XVI

Thy words have starkly told upon Us, but
Ill blood We would not breed, nor blooding can
We countenance on either hand. Perhaps
We are unable, yet Our order holds.

CAPTAIN DURLER

My King, I will not take this order hence
Before by scratch of cursive feather You
Have bled the royal name across its foot.

[*The King affixes His signature to the order. Exit Captain Durler with the order in hand.*]

MADAME ELIZABETH

What man of them tomorrow morn may pull
Him from his heavy sleep to draw once more
The soft and fragrant breath of summer's end?

CHABOT

[*Addressing the Assembly.*]
Be sure, the tide of revolution, sirs,
Is making high and must anon swill clean
The kettle France of ev'ry scrap and scum
Of tyranny.

MADAME ELIZABETH

[*Speaking in the earshot of those in the Reporter's box.*]
                    A figure ill-conceived,
I think. What is thy revolution, sir,
If not a draff with deputies afloat?
The honourable members as with peen
And pliers armed have set themselves to make
Another constitution. Solon speaks.

MERLET

Resolved and here adopted, gentlemen:
The King is now put down. The Monarchy,
As well the Constitution, is suspense.

KING LEWIS XVI

Will set the scribes of history down how that
The subjects self were such as brake and stilled
Their father's crownèd heart? Who may the ways
Of God unclew? What sins by this are swinged?

[*A tumult is heard from without the Assembly. Presently enter a madding throng of the populace carrying trophies of the fallen Tuileries. Some of the rioters carry over their shoulders the severed limbs of murdered Swiss Guards. One man holds in his bloody hands a ciborium containing the Most Blessed Sacrament. The trophies are piled on the President's desk. Some of the invaders shin up the columns to catch sight of the Royal Family in the Recorder's box. The deputies themselves are struck with terror.*]

A RIOTER

The blore, it blows; the blore it blows! Be King
No more, nor blood of princes be for aye.
We'll draw it forth and drink it off and belch
Like Harry Fee-Faw-Fum. Their grinded bones
Shall make the bread we cry. A *curse* of crowns!

ANOTHER RIOTER

[*Pointing to the Reporter's box.*]
We'll twain Him at the neck, say we, and have

His head upon a pike! Which done, we'll put
That trollop makeless 'neath the boultered blade.

A Third Rioter

Bring forth the royal monkeys; their regal brains
Need dashing out.
[*Addressing a female companion who has taken a pot from
his hands and furtively drinks from it.*]
                    Give 'ere that bleeding pot
Thou brinded cat! Beware a thirsty dog!

Merlet

All we assembled here applaud the zeal
Wherewith you speak your feeling voices full
Upon the want of flogging vice in kings
And courts. Yea, sev'ral of you speak both awe
And inspiration unto leaping hearts.
We beg to offer tribute of esteem
And vow to visit ev'ry evil wrought
Against the People. Know our fervid wish
That you may ev'ry confidence repose
In us. Howe'er, good citizens of France,
Your presence gladdens this Assembly, we
Your ministers agog to serve you as
Becomes a pious servant prompt upon
His master's wish and whim are bold to beg
Your leave to use all diligence required
Upon the business of the State, for which
You should from this Assembly take adieu.
By law it is that guilty blood is let.

A Rioter

What leave or law need we to let the life
Of blue-vein tyrants? Time it is to do
Red-handed carnage on our enemies.

Another Rioter

We wait upon your pleasure, gentlemen,
Against the happy moment when you seize
Them by the rising apple of their gulf.

[*Exeunt the rioters. As they leave, the following is heard:*]

A Third Rioter

T'was spoken *as* a gentleman, I'm sure!
[*Laughter is heard.*]
We only came to see that pursy kings
And barons proud should get their gruel. Scrag
'Em clean of life is what's to do, and soon.

A Fourth Rioter

Drag out the King, we say, the fair-necked Pen
As well, with all Her likely cygnets. Be
They tried and all be dead i' the swallow of
A sandglass! Quarter be there none before
They're lying sheeted corpses welt'ring in
Their ruddy lake of life at last, hee-hee!

[*Exeunt omnes, the Royal Family under guard.*]

Scene 5

[*In the Tower of the Temple, enter the King and M. William Christian de Malesherbes.*]

KING LEWIS XVI

My days to be are few. My life will soon
Be raft away of them intent that guilt
And innocence shall hang not on a deed
But on a state of life. No matter that,
Malesherbes; defense we shall pursue if sole
To let their touching or mine honour or
My name, conferred as by the pageant line
Of all the kings before me reigning. Far
Ago was cast my going off. My crime
Was to be crowned. I feel e'en now as done
Away. The blade's descent is preordained.

MALESHERBES

Against Your Majesty, Your enemies,
Distent of arrogance, so many big
But stuffless accusations have presumed
To bring, against all which my lords Tronchet,
De Sèze, and I will draw and loose at long.
The quiver rattles with three shining darts
And true to find and burst the swoll'n balloons.

KING LEWIS XVI

This new assembly, hight Convention, fore
Whose seat of mercy I shall take my trial
Immits on pain of death no murmur of

Exception; thus, my yestern confidents
Now study their survival, keeping mute—
A tonguelessness that eloquently speaks
A quailing meekness, as thou know'st, to dour
And cruel governance. Myself, my kin,
Thy country, shall for thy high valiance, that
As well of firm Tronchet and fast de Sèze,
Stand fixed in everlasting debt and deep.

    Thus much my wit has seized upon: if day
May dawn when crown and scepter grace again
This head, this hand, my duty sworn all else
Before will be to execute my God's
Request to consecrate this realm unto
His pierced and bleeding Heart for sinners—king
And Jacobin alike—aflame, so grant
Me grace and God's availing so to do.

Malesherbes

Than justice mete, I much regret to say,
Your hectic enemies would liefer spill
The regiment of kings, which palm to bear
They mean Your sacred person to mischieve.
But I, as well my watching colleagues—fate
And fashion staring out of countenance—
Will try amongst those heads untrothed as yet
To colder execution to arouse
And wake this wilderness of sleeping wit
By witchery of specious rhetoric
Long since o'erpoppied and abandoned to
The mimic thought of soothing dreams that draw
The walking sleeper to the precipice,
From which mere bias shaken he may vote

To spare a king—and France, in very deed.

King Lewis XVI

Need I remember thee, that bias there,
My Lord, runs passionate or terror drove?
If men say true, upon the bank o'er these
And ev'ry man that serves for deputy,
There sits a viewless spirit fierce and fell.
Caligula himself sat not more dread.
Its lancing tongue will lick the tremulous air;
Its scaly hood it throws. Its venom black
It spits at aught accused, not least at this. [*Pointing to Himself.*]

Malesherbes

Whose bodeful portrait, Sire, You pleased to give—
The Revolution's airy genius—
Is such a one as knocks, 'tis true, the spike
Of terror through the quick and core. No man—
No advocate—but inly joys to see
Its clients stupid from a previous
Exertion when before that Hall and hive
Of infamy a cause he comes to plead.

    Sometime, that grinning ghost that snarls in one
Or other revolutionary throat
May, casting round, take residence submerged
In denser substance, namely mortal flesh
Itself, which thence sole animate and owned
For ill, may do an universal hurt.

King Lewis XVI

I would not wake within thee, dear Malesherbes,
Untoward prospect. Much is yet to do
Ere loosing arrows. Lest mine eyes fall shut,
My heedless hand let fall this drooping pen,
It may our minds and sinews much behoove
To crawl away and court a dreamless rest.

Malesherbes

Forgive my pedant's rude prolixity.
We shall the arrows sharp and feather on
The morrow, an it please Your Majesty.

King Lewis XVI

To prayer and sleep and biding hope, my Lord.

[*Exeunt.*]

Scene 6

[*In the Hall of the Convention, thronged with deputies and spectators, enter the King; Raymond Romain, Count de Sèze; and Bertrand Barère, President of the Convention.*]

Bertrand Barère

Attend, deputed of the People's will.
It now remains for us, as President
Of this Convention, so to sum the case
Against th' accused as fervour like the fire

Of day might rise to melt and vapour drifts
Of ling'ring doubt and show where lies in bud
Your solemn duty to the Nation. First,
This Lewis, hight Capet, whilom King
Of France, made bold with criminal intent
Himself and ev'ry of his nearer kin
To take from lawful custody of that
Assembly then obtaining, driving swith
To reach that yonside standing deep in dire
Reaction, whence should march to drum and trump
The armies of that tyranny that till
This hopeful time has numbered centuries.

    As well, th' accused, whilst closely stayed of said
Assembly, furtively besought the help
Of friends without, all arrant foes and foul
Of Liberty and Nation. Unto some
He dared to offer royal patronage.

    As well, th' accused, in studied disregard
Of the Assembly, scrabbled cross a sheet
Intended for the blighted eyen of
A mitered enemy of man a vow
To grant again the freedom of the Church
If he, th' accused, should as before wield wide
The rod late fended by the People. Shall
The treble crown replace the single put
Forever to the ban these months agone—
The Phrygian cap be doffed in servile fear
Whene'er the stark biretta passes? Foh!
[*Pointing to the King.*]
    Was't not in wise of th' tow'ring tyrant oak,
He spread abroad a canopy of pow'r
To shadow all the green and whispering hopes

About his base lest they more leave and bloom
Than miserable subject weeds? Not less.

    As well, I say, th' accused, a laggard to
The last, waxed temerarious and spake
Most shocking scorn and detestation of
The Constitution. More, he did his might
To thwart its spirit, being bold t' impose
The odious veto on the People's will.

    More shocking *toto coelo*, citizens,
Th' accused, become a brand and makestrife, did
Devise and instigate the rising on
The tenth of August last full sure as he
Had laid his crusted scepter down and rung
The tocsin with his self and horrid hand!

    Of evidence, we say, what need you more?
We rest the Prosecution, knowing well
Your zeal for probity and justice done.

    This Chair herewith invites the citizen
De Sèze to rise and say again in short
His client's vindication; whereupon,
This house will weigh and sift and thence pronounce.

Count de Sèze

[*Rising and facing the Convention.*]
I thank the Chair, to which and unto you,
O citizens, I can but own in sooth
My vainly weening how these jaded ears
Had heard the sum of frivolous charges men
Have brought before the weary courts of law.
I erred. This final accusation now
Pronounced so levies tributary faith
As it should beggar rank credulity.

The charge implies th' accused exculpate both
From this and ev'ry else impeachment brought;
For if the King did soothly instigate
A general insurrection 'gainst Himself,
He stands a lunatic immune, as such,
From prosecution of whatever kind.

    An honest man will needs say out that in
This very hall some deputies have played
The pretty braggart's prize for e'en the name
Of master architect of August ten.
The other sev'ral charges here rehearsed
Are every one undue. Th' accused—quite sane—
Stands fair and should stand free of all attaint.
Address we first that flight of the accused,
His wife and nearest kin in desperate train.

    In gross defiance of the laws of France,
The King, for so He was, dear citizens,
Was jailed, and thus He long remained, without
A charge against Him brought, no trial convened,
Or verdict spoke. A name there is for such
Confinement, learned sirs; it is duress.
It may be asked by heads giv'n something o'er
To thought what duty to His captors owed
The King. I put it to you citizens,
He owed them sole the dust upon His shoon.
From God and th' common oath of kings, He had
In charge to slip the iron hobbles of
Injustice, e'vn the violation of
His sacred person, not to say the Queen's,
The Dolphin's, and the Princess Royal's. Hence,
Deliverance was all Their deed though in
Event Their happy bourne of refuge had

As well been shimmering as a looming yond
The ev'ry-coloured bow of Heaven's blue.

    Address we next the charge of patronage,
A charge wherein, as well, sobriety
And sense are all to seek. What man could fail,
Without a sounding censure's crims'ning
His selfish ears, to aid a friend in straits
Who once had served him when to serve had brought
The server into danger, calling forth
His fellows shrills of dudgeon, even threats
Of death? Is selfless loyalty to go
A-begging in the dispensation new?

    And what though bishops by their king should be
Protected, who have proved at impious hands
An hypocritic persecution? Pray,
Is Liberty your law? Then, wherefore bar
The Church from feeding hungry men their bread
Of consolation? Vowing freedom to
Restore to ministers of Heaven's grace,
The King was sole about the solemn cure
That has from king to king since Clovis crowned
Succeeded to this present. Duty called
A king to duty wed; need more be told?

    Now, gentles—citizens—(pray grant me shrift),
True 'tis the Constitution much misliked
The King; I beg your leave to urge, howe'er,
How breathless zeal upon this matter has
('Twas ever thus) outstripped discernment. Would
A sober, civic head expect the King
To like the Constitution, under which
These sev'ral months He has been languishing
A prisoner? Shall it be a crime to like

Or not? Though He had paced a dirge through all
Its nice provisions, must He stand in doom
For that? With trick of reasonable paint
A further charge scarce worth a smile is laid
Full thickly on wherein th' accused presumed
To exercise the veto writ within
The Constitution. What the law supreme
Allows must in the use be deemed a crime!
Now lunacy is law, and history
May tell how then-a-days a willful crank
Could be saluted as Lycurgus' self.
    In fine, O men, think well and long how tongues
And chronicles the ages down will all
This tale of broil and tumult story. When,
That door set wide, this chamber I surveyed
I saw not judges, but accusers, some
Of whom looked harriers, fierce and loud in cry.
Excuse yourselves from judgement and acquit
Your King discrowned, the innocent of these
Accuses. Rather, ask what honour have
The nations, absent cause, to make away
With kings? This case, flown forth a viewless tongue's
Fork end can little bear inspection. Hence,
The Prosecution hies you headlong to
A verdict green and crude this darksome day.

[*Exit the Count de Sèze after bowing to the President's
Chair. Exit the King under guard.*]

Scene 7

[Into a room in the Tower of the Temple, enter the King and M. Cléry, His valet de chambre.]

King Lewis XVI

I know not why the turnkeys yet will not
Immit Maleherbes. They meanly joy, I ween,
In whatso discommodes the prisoner's strife
To live one day to next—or ere they drag
Him hence in chains to give upon his neck.

Cléry

Oh Sire, say other. Sure it is that much
Of those assembled hearts will sup them on
The honey of compunction and absent
Them from that hive of angry votes, left thence
Without enough of venom as may stun
The staggering mayfly, much less or Yourself
Or France. A plague of raging bees and wasps!

King Lewis XVI

Cléry, death's step alarms me nothing; I
Have manned myself to dissolution. Sure,
Thou know'st my soul will wisp anon away.
What use to cry upon them harrow now?

Cléry

Your Majesty, in solemn spectacle
There nighs this where of woe a sober train
Whose faces wan and speak them heavy with

A charge of words. Oh God, the heart strikes fast!

[*Enter, led by Philip Antony Grouvelle and Dominic Joseph Garat, a deputation from the Convention. Facing them, the King strikes a noble and imposing attitude.*]

GARAT

[*His hat on his head.*]
By them we serve, O Lewis, we are bid
To read thee their decree whilere set down.

GROUVELLE

[*Speaking in a weak and trembling voice.*]
The National Convention here declares
Thee, Lewis Capet, last ensceptered king
Of th' French convict of plots to make against
The Nation's liberty, for which delict
Most grave thou shalt before the clock from hence
Tells twenty-four ascend the altar of
The People, there to lay thy length and die
Beneath their flashing indignation's steel.

KING LEWIS XVI

[*The King steps forward; takes the decree from Grouvelle; folds it; and, removing a portfolio from His pocket, places the document in it. From the portfolio He draws out a letter and offers it to Garat.*]
Lord Minister of Justice, know that with
This missive I beseech three days' delay
That 'gainst the appointed execution of
The sentence capital I might prepare

Me to appear before Almighty God.
    I ask an end of all the ceaseless search
And watch of peering eyes, the organs of
A black and bulking imbecility
That shadows on my mind, which wants the rays
Of reason's tranquil recollection. More,
I pray that curtained in confinement I
May ere my doomed and fixèd going hence
Be reunited with my kindred near.
    I much desire the said Convention to
Address, and soon, the disposition of
These hearts, of nothing guilty save their kin
To one convict. Let not that body reach
Its wrath at them, but reach them freedom from
This breathless close of stone and iron. I
Commend all others that have served me to
The Nation's care, who stand from now in need.

GARAT

Thy letter, sir, I will deliver quite
As thou requestest. More I may not do.

KING LEWIS XVI

[*Drawing a scrip from His pocket.*]
This paper speaks the name and place of one
In bands I wish to guide me unto God.

[*He hands it to Garat. Exit Garat, followed by the others
of the deputation. Exeunt the King and M. Cléry.*]

Scene 8

[*Into a room in the Tower of the Temple, enter the King and M. Cléry.*]

KING LEWIS XVI

Intelligence I have, Cléry, how I
Must yet be headed on the morrow. Lo,
Where comes a dreadful hour of weeping.

[*Enter the Queen, the Dauphin, the Dauphine, and Madame Elizabeth. Exit M. Cléry after bowing to all. The King sits down, the Queen on His left, Madame Elizabeth on His right, the Dauphine nearly opposite to Him, and the Dauphin between His knees. All bend towards Him and hold Him half embraced.*]

                                                   Come
My wedded dove and sweetings all, that I
Might fold you to my heart while yet it beats.
My Queen, my lambs, oh dearest unto me
In all the world, upon the morrow morn
This writhen soul must vapour forth to meet
The radiant Son of God on high, Whose Heart
Of flames alight will not be stayed or 'scaped.

[*The Queen and all the others who have entered cry out and wail pitiably.*]

QUEEN MARY ANTOINETTE

Oh, sentence brute and bittermost! Oh, scourge

Of God thy judges; sure, of nothing have
They shame! Now wan, my heart, and wither. I
Will ne'er be buoyed of man nor blithesome more.

King Lewis XVI

Say not intemp'rately. Our state as King
And Queen and th' Paragon of kings above
Us bind Us to an inward poise. Not all
Of men are wolves and jackals—eaters all
Of broken meats—if few be seraphs true
And sainted. Let our brows be smooth, our eyes
Unshot with dudgeon's blood. Be thou the Queen.
As well, my children, quit ye down the years
As royals; unto nothing common stoop.
Christ grace you; Charlemagne defend you; clad
You in the purest plate Saint Lewis crowned!

Madame Elizabeth

[*Pointing to the door.*]
Sweet Lewis, these a heavy freight of guilt
Shall bear, whose sins from son to son will sure
Succeed. The brethren trowelled and aproned all—
Perhap thy cousin self, nay treason's self—
Will noint themselves wi' th' blood of royals to claim
The honorific Kings of Regicide.
In treachery not Brutus was their peer.
Though these obtain, th' avenging harpy forth
Their desperate jaws will wrench the slathered meats
Of victory to leave them hung'ring still,
Bereft with blood beneath their squalid nails.

Queen Mary Antoinette

Oh God, that we might all be wizarded
To happier times, the fleeted years and gone!
That we might see again the land in leaf,
France one in faith and chivalrous in deed.

The Dauphin

Dear Papa, shall we never hug thee more?
I should so glad to tarry here within
Thy circling arm and next thy loving heart.
I dare be sworn how dearest Maman, dear
Elizabeth, and I have numbered dark
And chill a thousand days below. The guards
Are ever throwing jibes and scorns at us.
Oft floating in their cups, they reckon me
With cold and squinting eye and offer with
Batoon to swinge me for a shiv'ring cur.
I back from them but look them hard withal.

King Lewis XVI

[*Brushing and straightening the Dauphin's somewhat
ragged clothes.*]
Behold my dearest son and brave beyond
His boyish years! On thee from now should fall
The cope of kings, the Cap of State. 'Twere thine
To balm and bind the staring wounds of France.

The Dauphin

I would be like to thee, dear Papa, wise
And good—to everyone a father sworn.

King Lewis XVI

I would I had been so, my child. 'Tis God's
To judge this heart's unworth. Comport thee as
A king, or stayed dark months within this tow'r
Or throned one lightsome day in palaces
Afar. Give thee His grace the latter once
To be. Fore all, embrace whate'er He please
To send for thy improving. Tissue all
Thy days with golden threads of Charity
That vested o'er with gold thou may'st be crowned
With cross and flow'rs of everlasting life.

Queen Mary Antoinette

[*Speaking through tears and sobs.*]
My temples strike; my heart is hardly vised
With grief; assurgent terrors teem and crowd
Upon us long the days.
[*Turning to the door and addressing the absent Convention.*]
                              Ye parricides!
Ye brutal! Ye flown to lip with blackest bile
And arrogance! Oh, save us God from these!
[*She weeps violently.*]

King Lewis XVI

Sweet wife, reel not abroad thy wonted pale
Of self-possession. Give no more; thou must
Unfair thy face. Do on the courage of
A Queen and number not our miseries.
Put not a draft upon thy sanity,
But dry these fonts of scalding wretchedness.
For very much betimes, all we shall band

In sweetest bliss above, when tears will fleet
For e'er away in noon of radiant joy.

THE DAUPHINE

Oh, Papa, though thou mak'st to visit us
With comfortable words, thy kindness makes
Us miserable more, whereof we shall
Be soon bereft upon this heartless waste.
Oh, let me rather fare away with thee.

KING LEWIS XVI

And leave Maman in desolation lorn?
Thou must remain to hearten her, to hold
Thy brother's artless hand and be his map's
Own flower of the winds along this life.

THE DAUPHINE

Thy will shall wing the arrow of my days;
No wish of thine, dear Father, shall I fail
Grant God the waft of His unfading grace.

KING LEWIS XVI

[*The King rises.*]
My Mary, children thrice and more beloved,
Elizabeth, my better mind and soul
Of sanity, the good Abbé awaits
Above to ready me and shrive me 'gainst
The morrow do of sad decree. Be sured
How at the strike of seven next we shall
Once more be met to give the last adieus.

QUEEN MARY ANTOINETTE AND THE OTHERS

[*In tears and moaning.*]
You promise us?

KING LEWIS XVI

I promise ye, sweet kins.
[*Very expressively.*]
Adieu.

[*The sobs redouble. Enter M. Cléry. The Queen holds the King by the right arm; each gives a hand to the Dauphin; the Dauphine on the left clasps the King's body; Madame Elizabeth, on the same side but a little behind the rest, catches the left arm of the King. They make a few steps towards the entrance, uttering the most sorrowful moans. The Dauphine faints at the King's feet, which she clasps. Cléry raises her and helps Madame Elizabeth hold her.*]

KING LEWIS XVI

Arise, poor flow'r, O fade of face. Pray speak
Her gently up. The cups of sorrow are
Fulfilled. Weep out thy sadness now and sleep.

[*Exeunt M. Cléry, the Queen, the Dauphin, the Dauphine, and Madame Elizabeth. Exit the King.*]

Scene 9

[*Enter a coach into the Place Lewis XV, populated by what should suggest a vast throng, including many guards and*

drummers drumming. A scaffold with the guillotine stands at
the center. From the coach, exeunt guards; the King; and His
confessor, the Abbé Edgeworth de Firmont.]

King Lewis XVI

So, finally forth, my dear Abbé, to tinct
The boards beneath this flying pageant of
The sky. There opens to the view a mad
Misrule. The vast assembled seem to breathe
With awful intuition. They as well
Are come to be themselves beheaded here.
[*Addressing the guards.*]
    When ye have done, pray use this good Abbé
With all respect, to whom We greatly owe
Our readied state of soul this heavy day.

[*Three brutish executioners rush to the King to remove*
His coat.]

King Lewis XVI

Now enter energumens. Stand away!
[*The King thrusts them back and undoes His collar*
and shirt.]
    I need no busy valets here. Relent!
[*They make to tie His hands.*]
Tie Us! You shall not. Once and swift away
That blade beneath 'twill be and soon enough.

Abbé Edgeworth de Firmont

Fall not, Your Majesty, at caustic words.
Along the curling lip of this contempt

For You, I see the Lamb in patience bear
His Cross, inviting You to like more near
His Heart, but beats from now Your quittance high
Aloft such men as unto murder grown
Propense have named their King a criminal.

King Lewis XVI

Indeed, 'tis this alone, thy vision, can
Induce my resignation to so base
An outrage. Now be thorns Our Cap of State.
[*To the executioners.*]
    Whatso ye wish then do. The chalice will
We drain this day to e'en the bitterest dregs.
[*The executioners tie His hands behind Him and lead Him to the scaffold. He mounts the steps.*]
    O Death, to thee I pace a swift approach.

Abbé Edgeworth de Firmont

O Son of sainted Lewis, rise to Heav'n!

[*Reaching the platform of the scaffold and inspired by the words of the Abbé, the King escapes the executioners; rushes to the edge of the platform; and, motioning the drummers to be silent, addresses the crowd in a tremendous voice.*]

King Lewis XVI

Ye citizens of France discrowned, We stand
Quite innocent of all the tedium
Of charges—every one untenable—
Of which We come convict. Ye know Us as
Your father long your advocate with God,

Your shield, as well, to ward the selfish use
Of men more set on pow'r and gold than good.
We here forgive the wights—whose conscience seems
By day and day to peak and wither—that
Have sadly severed Us from you. Not less,
We pardon their intent to sunder fore
The world Our soul and body, and We pray
Our spout of blood may not upon your heads
Descend or find and mar the hearths and fields
Of France, whose soul fetch God from terrors now
And ever forth this...

COMMANDER OF THE GUARD

[*On horseback and crying ferociously.*]
                         Sound the drums, ye dogs!
And nothing droop. Let every jack stand fast.

[*Forthwith, the executioners seize the King and drag Him under the axe of the guillotine. The blade falls and the crowd roars. A curtain immediately falls. At the same moment and rising quite above this sound is heard a large choir of singers performing the chorus "Worthy Is the Lamb" from Handel's* Messiah.]

A YOUNG POET'S ELEGY TO THE COURT OF GOD

Part the First

Ye blessed gods created and sublimed
Of God, ye suns who far out-throng the flue
Of winding stars borne round upon the breathed,
Irrefragable Word, ye swiftly bear
Us frailties His gracious errands; and like
Alcyone alit upon the spelled,
Obedient flood of death ye brood the clutch
Of riping souls with feathered panoplies
Of musky wings becrimsoned deep and fair
As the ruffled rose. The while—oh mystery!
Ye shelter far aloft the glittering vaults
Of night to worship fixed as golden bees
In amber or rapt as the sovran bird that lifts
By noon to the fresh, annunciating winds
And glances undestroyed the flames and beams
Of the ramping sun (though other eyes and proud
Were mazed and, like Semele entoiled, struck bolt
In ashes). Oh, attend mine instant pray'rs,
Ye interceding angels, especially thou,
Mine Angel Guardian; for, except your love

With orant flame alight shall magnify
My poor beseechments unto God, they must
In the white, exceeding brilliancy of Heav'n
Soon faint and 'clipse.

    Atop youth's ridge, upon that headland scar
That fronts the tide of ev'ry wending wight's
Majority, I stand a poet born,
A staved and girded pilgrim hitherwards
Attaining from my native close, where first
I pulled the milk of mercy and delight:
My perdurable Catholic faith and all
The living wonts and uses quick it there
Has incarnated time all out of mind.
Below me now I gaze the sighing surf,
Whose fingers smoothe the beaten sand and draw
The shipmen to her. Like the bards, or great
Or small, that have preceded me and dared
The shrug of Ocean, I must soon embark
And, making sail upon the flood, run straight
For Parnasse and the font of Castaly.

    I cry upon your sanctitudes to stand
The patrons of my humble pen, for ye
Lay hold upon this various world at once
By always very intuitions, which
Themselves as swiftly rapture *you*. As soon
As thriven bees in rose-bloom ye cast mature
From out the Mind of God, ye cataphracts
As bright as living steel. For ye were not
As who in gentle arm lie hard at suck
And staring on their mindful mothers' eyes.
Nor o'er ye spirits inextense did time
Bear sway, whose pointing tipstaff monishes

Us flesh with fretful taps and larums shrill
How we will dote upon the drowsy charms
Of indolence. Nor yet were ye become
A blighted purlieu to the hob of death,
The sneering, brute familiar that swags
The flesh and fuddles the mind until at glint
Of folding star he shears the lifestrings through
And, being jaded, casts his broken toys
Upon the sleeping dust. But though our souls
Be still at war with self and Hell and, so,
Must offer frequent battle—sometime close
With hideous shape in passage fierce of arms—
'Tis not of grim testudo or the fell
Goliath we are threated—our enemies
All met in reeking, undivided sum
And making boldly at us all at once.
And are we wounded in a sore attempt
And collied, indeed are rived and fall'n amidst
Our ruddy spilth of life, we make our shrift
In tears and rise God's paladins, once more
By grace to stand Hell's blatant emp'ry at
Defiance. But on your *own* trial's battlestead
How brief your sojourn, yet how hard withal!
To bear salvation's palm all ye must wage
Each one his sword of grace against his own
Armipotent and self-sufficient wraith
And shend him with one stroke or lose the day
And day eternal—in plain, must unto God
All utterly and instantly commend
Yourselves or from His proffered graces shrink
Indign and cold, endungeoning yourselves
Within the oubliette of self for ay.

So at your thronging forth, th' Almighty God
At once enshrouded ye within the grey
Sequester of a swaddling cloud; for did
Ye front the glory of your sudden God,
Ye must, unwilled and meritless, have drawn
To Him annihilate, like iron crumbles
Twitched dumb to th' imperious magnet. Unto you
Free will He gave and now would prove your faith,
Who whisperèd ye thus: "Our firstlings paled,
Whose self-adverting eyen survey and take
Your inward deeps suspense with all the types
Of Our creation, yield your majesties
To Us, the fiery vast of love, Who will
Not mete, how far soe'er your heated hearts
May urge therein their coltish way and pure.
Come unto Us now rathe and with a will
And rest within Our circling fathom still."
   What tided now, alas, could show no more
To frighted mortal stare than summer's bluff
And elemental greenman, what virid storm
Rebukes aloud the panic vales and strings
Against the sweeping winds a jagged warp
Of fire. For straight upon these words of grace,
There pealed from angel hearts such rhapsody
Of multitudinous praise as here upon
This puisne earth had ravished Typhon from
His wits and made Briareus' heart strike wild.
Then into Heaven ye were haled as flights
And headlong tides of sheeting flame, such fire
As earthly dread might take for levin swords
Wherewith the Lord must hew in shreds the pearled
And diamonded stole of night, or else

For glowing trees wherewith He fain would blind
The single eye of cyclopean day.
To sainted eyes and ears initiate these
High prodigies, wherein of tried ye were
Become triumphant, sure had been those things
They were: th' eternal liturgy of Heav'n
And blaze of your transfiguration. They
Had drawn the blameless, prisoned soul on earth
As if she were the powdered moth of May
That nightlong watching i' the closet's dim
Shall mad against the panes and lattices
Serenely lighted of the fulling moon.
    Ne ev'ry angel was advanced above
His natural rise; for, ere your Hold and Hearth
Thus triced you into Heaven, frigid pride,
Your brethren meanly grand and failing shame,
Of Love Divine thought quiet scorn and like
The whisperous wind that or the tempest rage
Will hunt the trees their crowding, signal leaves
To whelm, they lipped, each one, "I will not serve."
Whom God All Just thereat disprinced and to
The thirsting mouth of Hell at once threw down
Like slant and thunderbolted torrents. Thence
He first in pride, the blackened webster of
A thousand wiles, would sway our parents first
Create and then dispatch amongst their seed
All his dark inclining, who each, against
The universal doom be trumped, must lure
His chase to fool its little span of life
Away and thus to suffer inward rot.
And like the maculate beast that stirs what time
The sun lies bleeding on the western hills,

Each fiend at liberty amongst the stiff
And grinning swath of scything death shall nose
The air for ghostly carrion until
With bloody jaws and sagging belly he
Shall last at Dawn away. Defend us, God!
    But like a mighty air, the Paraclete
Dispersed th' occulting mists, which hurled as hush
And swift away as rack at tempest's end.
And thus th' Almighty God in countenance
Of unconcealèd fire and radiant
The reach of Heaven's aery climates now
Was pleased to luminate, to Whom ye quired
Your everlasting hymn like them that wide
Away in copse and meadow rise from brier
And trailing weed to thrill in stabs of bliss
Their morning canticles of praise unto
The fecundating sun. And from the siege
Of holy radiance the Triune God
Decreed the many-marbled world, all which
Upon ye angels peered in stroke of fly's
Wing, clean from nought both floor of earth and vault
Of sable sky, which after blazoning
With hue of azure day He bossed and swagged
With silver stars and glowing galaxies.
Within this glittering flood of time and space,
A vastity that unto God must like
Unto a solid moment scarcely more
Of bulk than sprite's incorporeity,
All living things should thence by slow degrees
And measurable goings or stand upon
A course for home or fetch away to wrack.
    Behold, ye dreadless Host! by God ordained

To governors, shields, and sentinels, at His
Cathedral charge ye lively drave abroad
The universe to wind the galaxies
In great siderial roundelays of laud.
But soft! Forgive these feeble numbers; here
A poet's fancy must to man's five wits
Less rudely character profundity.
These eyes, by Thomas schooled, have late descried
Of your so careful tasks, the awful kind,
Which now my love begs suff'rance to rehearse.
Whenas the Lord upon the moment thought
Ye into being, He willed of passing love
That, since ye would anon by grace approve
Yourselves His children, all ye should have part
In His creative facts to come. And thus
He found ye full with all th' ideas of
The myriad universe yet uncreate,
Each lapped as tight as winter bud against
Such providential hour as it should quite
Disclose itself to the bare advertence of
Your ardent gaze and blow within your pied
Academies of perfect lore. So soon
As ye their fastness glance to flower by one
And sundry through the while of time, so soon
Their answerable beings show i' the void
Like fairy rings upon the green, as if
Ye breathed from blows immortal tufted crops
Of seed upon a wild and raised therefrom
A brief display of thurible flow'rs to cense
The courts of gold and silver light. At once
In foal new thrown nor licked ye contemplate
The crumping, belted horse; in strew of mast

The stand of oak in all detail ye scry.
And by such intuitions real as fair,
And in the Lord's creative thought subsumed,
Ye still breed up His creatures animate,
Wherewith the fleshed and foliated world
Ye swarm anew. In doings thus exalt
Are limned your more than tutelary pow'rs
Of God our Lord all generous conferred.
   In midst the new-struck fires that stately foot
Their pavans cross the upward night, the earth
Entire must now a swung incensory
Become and breathe to its Creator fumes
Of all the grains and gums of life. Upon
Its min'ral ground of hunched and splitten rock
Involving inchmeal o'er a hectic melt
Th' Omnipotent His handiwork fulfilled
By step and step twixt patient being and
Your legion selves, who yet at once were made
More divers far than all through land and sea
Should teem and tribe. At first, and as alway
With your partaking charactered e'vn now,
He formed the merely vital beings, who
To magnify their Gardener but grope
The yielding clods and bush to the cordial sun.
Thereon, He fashioned beings sensitive
And vital both, who in miaul, chirp, blate,
Or squeal their Lord unthought will brutely praise.
   Now waxing much of expectation's warmth,
Ye mantled o'er with charitable joy;
For that ye knew of God that He would soon
The parent of the thrice-ensoulèd race
Of men create, whose inches forth the slime

Of earth He promptly spoke. And having strung
The bones with brawn, and shaped a folden brain,
He thereunto inspired a viewless ghost,
A ghost needs rational; for e'vn as all
Ye unembodied spirits shall be full
Intuitive, so spirits into gross
Extension breathed must unto discourse set
Their lab'ring pow'rs that they may come to know
And thenceforth love and serve their God. Within
This robe of clay the senses thorough time
But victual each the puzzling wits of men
With incremental crusts of sensibles,
Who therewithal must ever fetch and try
Conclusions, which we pray full just may stand.
Now wrenching forth our eldest patriarch
A ruddy rib, th' Almighty God shaped out
Thereof the mother of our race and did
Our parents twain to know His holy Will—
How they should quite abstain their lips from fruit
Of the inviolable tree and thus
Receive eternity of joy at gaze
Upon His beatific Face. Alas,
The Sire of Lies had parted, but not 'scaped,
His everlasting dog-hole and, afoot
Upon the earth, would speak our parents fair
And breathe upon their burnished souls; for sight
Of simple-hearted innocence so greened
His sober gravity as he must snarl
This happy world and swear it of the courts
Of Hell. While yet he curled like kindling in
The roar of Hell's own writhing flames, he coiled
Him into serpent's form and, lancing oft

His cloven tongue the tremulous air to prove,
He nigh our mother drew his odious shape.
With addle heart, but hatching mind, he speaks
Her fair and has, an she but taste of the
Innominable fruit, how she must rise
A goddess, knowing good and ill, and paints
Unto her prompt imagination all
The vanities that since have cozened us,
Her numb'rous strain. At length, come stupid with
The fumes of flattery and sadly flush
With visions of her deity, she could
Not find her pow'r of will; whereon she culled
And tasted. Nor our father better fared.
Albe his spouse's guilt had put him to
A momentary stand, he also, at
Her eager suasion, fleshed his appetite
And on his flagrant head and progeny
Plucked death and ev'ry evil else that here
Lays scourge cross human soul and body. Thus
So far ago the universal mar
Was wrought. Instead of drawing skyward in
Apotheosis, our wretched parents were
Bedwarfed in wringing cramps of guilt and shame.
    But though proudblooded Lucifer and's toads
Acrouch had at their own depravities
Been into lava briskly poled, the Lord
Vouchsafed to spare our parents fall'n. Perchance
They misdemeaned something backward of
Consent or somehow failed to seize of that
They did the deadly gravity. In fine,
Perhaps their being in the flesh was why
All Mercy deigned betimes to grant them and

Their offspring place and long occasion yet
To ripen through His grace for life eterne.
And so against the swoop of the ringing scythe,
Alike the corn and cockle swell within
God's croft of mortal men. But ere killed hearts
Abroad the world might life unhoped obtain
Within His love, th' immeasurable due
Of expiation must be rendered. Thus,
To ev'ry man should ever live He vouched
A Saviour in His only Son begot,
Who came far other than the conqueror
The Chosen waited. For to quit our souls
Of ev'ry chain and iron hamper and
To everlasting peace redeem us home,
He suffered the indignant world to do
Him unto death upon a gallows tree.
Though long since risen from the jealous grave,
He yet stays clenched to this our very tree
Of knowledge and, in this meek attitude,
Descends the suppliant morn to be the Bread
Of our redemption; as well His Sacred Heart
Afire upon the altar urges forth
His Wounds the oozing, infinite measure of
His Blood, our Drink of ever-during life.

 O Jesu, grant that as St. George I might
Each day address my heart in tabard white
Emblazed with sign of those two boards across
And soaken red with Thy most precious Blood
And that sustained of Thy sweet Sacrament
Might rive the monsters on my way to Thee.

Part the Second

And ye, sweet messengers, ye ninefold at
The ready ministration of your King,
I shall at long pore out mine eyes upon
This glancing sea. How mightily it throws
At this bare, monumental pitch of rock
Whereon I stand! Years since, I put my muse
To reason's goodly school as, next the flame
That bows and dances o'er the scholar's lamp,
I spent away the careful hours of
My nonage. Hitherunto having bent
My plodding, philosophic way, by great
Divines and sages ever lit, I last
Attained to this commanding prospect of
The sea, the vast variety of all
That seems. Now as I late was bold to breathe,
I wish, oh humbly! so it be to God
Agreeable, to lay a course below
This steep for Parnasse and the coronal
Of leaves that rounds the poet's brow beyond
This mobile world of greedy multitude.
We painful heads will thrash and riddle from
Particularities their gen'ral truths,
Which when abstract beneath our bleaching gaze
Will want a savour and completeness. But
The Source of Truth, preventing hollow need
Has gently bidden divers men to lay
For all our starveling selves the feast of art.
From out th' innumerality that throngs
Upon our senses five, th' Almighty deigns
Such elements to fish as may be oned

To make a fable, strain, or comely shape,
Each in its kind reflecting His so brave
Creation—each an airy unity
Of gen'ral notion and particular
Example. All as in a ringing forge
These likenesses He roundly works as if
By hammerstroke and 'midst the answ'ring spill
Of candent sparks and showery flakes of fire.
This glowing handiwork, for men ordained,
To which, by grace, ye deftly ply your own
Creative hands, ye swiftly bear to who
In patience stay the sudden blaze of art.
Each semblance casts a fervid influence
That renders mortal mind and heart as flush
As fired steel and straight atones them in
A dazzling ecstasy. And so the Lord,
By playing fantasies on inward eye
And ear of artist intermedial,
To mankind gives that, like ye thunderlights
At intuition's stroke (who have, nor need,
Imagination), they should see and love
At once—should apprehend abiding truths
While corporate full in graceful blows of act
Or substance. Though such flow'rs be fictive shapes
They own to mortal eyes more perfect or
More present symmetries reflecting His
Eternal Truth than e'er things unideal
May cede. And unto reason's work, which likes
Unto a moil of ants at prising of
The folded peony, those jealous flow'rs
And wry of actual creation do
But loathly yield their crabbed truths. And sure,

When discourse hales his prisoners abstract
To human gaze, they show them ghosts of wan
And stuffless kind. A tale exalt or touch
Of golden wires shall limn the Universe
More throughly than a lab'ring discourse or
A slate of formularies cramped. Than dull
Descriptions oils and marbles are more worth.
For art persuades the soul and toles her rapt
To everlasting life. Thus, perfect truths
Of visionary source alone beneath
The moon our blinkard understanding both
And promptly glad and breed. Oh, out of count
The number of His clemencies! How much
The scend of His beneficence, Who thus
Our souls with darts of joy will still traverse!

    Wherefore, ye streaming light of joy in truth,
I now unto my knees am fallen least
Of men to beg that in the torrent of
Your unremitting prayer ye would beseech
My Lord to send me by my Guardian true
The plotted charts of visionary tales
That unto humankind might character
The very world. And thou, my cherished Friend
And Minister, pray compass me about
When from this lofty brow of granite I
Shall urge my downward way and go amongst
My peers, who now discalced in whispered airs
And mild slow foot a many-dimpled trace
Upon the sodden verge of sand. They fare
From yond maternal harbour's gentle clasp,
Wherein they spent the golden light of this
Now silvering day in trimming everyone

His craft careened upon the dry and for
The near salt wave athirst. Myself, betimes,
Must slightly farther pilgrim to mine own
Dear craft beneath to brace her helm and scrape
Her crusted keel, to scan her cloth, and all
Her boatlong seams to pay full thick against
Their making water i' the tempest. When
I have dispatched these works and so thou shalt
Have brought that grace for which I e'vn now prayed
The Quires' high intercession, do thou deign
To hover o'er the mast and, as thou wast
A painted wind distent of cheek, bag forth
The beggar sails in crimson signed that soon
And long my prow of gaze serene might cleave
The panic of shouting foam and leaping waves
Upon the main. No Christian poet but
Avers that actions plotted down in tales
From Heav'n must have him scatheless to that leaved
And bloomy Mount of truths perennial.
    Remark now, Angel, how those bards go thence
To take their rest; they act as sure as gods.
(And so do I, I trow, thy little charge!)
Just so, I fancy, young Poseidon smoothed
And bridled the dolphin sea, fawning at
His sooth command. My ready watchman's glance
Flown forth this shore of my absorption shows
Me that the moon upon her mystic round
Has coaxed the shallows from their oozy bed.
But lo! what melancholy ruin is
Discovered to mine eyes? I barely make
Upon that mire the black remain of what
Was erst a worthy craft and sleek. How did

Her master helm her to this shape? Indeed,
I fear a shape delusory, if fair,
Was calved and made to witch his heart away
Until he drave upon a rock and quit
These wooden bones to worm and water. Oh,
Methinks I hear the beams cry out and split
Asunder! Oh, he casts him monstrous on
The fluid mercies of the sea! 'Tis true
No bane will visit who shall wightly stand
Upon his course; but ere we poets young
Have squared the yards—before we yet have laid
Our noble tales abroad—we oft conceit
That we can breast the heaving ocean in
The cockle self-reliance and elude
The jagged mouths that lie agape beneath
The doubtful wave. Let all high-crested youth
Would fain strike o'er the surge bethink themselves
That, ere our eldest Parents fetched away
To wrack, that undersea extending far
Beyond the plummeting of mortal eyes
Was long the habitation of the bad.
O thou my Lamp celestial and all
Ye firmament of light, who condescend
To be our votive fires, ye know that these
Malign within the green abysm are
The very demonry disfellowed from
Your consort ages since. They count below
As many as the sumless grails that shroud
The beds of the interminable seas.
Ye also know that all this main is but
The welter of myself, and any self
Resolved as I to fetch the land beyond

The misty verge of straining human sight.
  In Greekish myth was blindly storied just
Such one as they that through these waters swim
To work destruction still. I speak of whom
Th' uncircumcised called Phorcus, him they might
Have named base sire of monsters; sea-god spawned
Of Hell; dim, diabolic libertine.
Now into dreadful Ceto, nearest of
His sib, he threw his wanton seed, whereat
She bulked prodigious as she swum the flood;
And like the schooling cows that crawl from out
The waves in spring, she last lay shuddering on
The strand and dropped a get of freaks that roamed
The frighted world and plagued the souls of men.
The cursed originals of Phorcus black,
Those more black moving in the deeps, still bend
Themselves to troll us shipmen from our course.
The poet's self, as any else's, would
To knowledge, pow'r, or mere sensation slave
Him, though he ne'er so gravely don the cap
Of manumission. But those Argus eyes,
His quiet lodgers, know that gladliest
He would but feel and verse his feelings to
The nerves of other men, for all he feed
Nor form will, intellect, or character,
Be they as shrinkshanks gone a begging with
The empty bowl. Thus, from the running throngs
That by his mind's five tributary locks
Attain his oceanic self, the fiends
Will seize perceptions apt and get upon
Them all such symbols or adventures as
Should answer his ignoble bent. No trope

Or action thus begot will ever show
Or story him the truth that he must go
Abroad himself and that along his gift
Of days, though he shall sometime federate
And sometime measure with the world externe,
'Tis sole above the wash he has his grace
And wends him fain to home and Father. Nay,
Like Ceto's whelp, Echidna, bold upon
The ocean, these perfidious calves of Hell
Will float all fair and sleek above the wave
Whilst coiling horrid all below it. How
So long the faring bard shall stand upon
His course, these monsters will lay wait for him
And rise like naiads from the glittering seas
About his keel that by impostures they
Might reach him from his high resolve and draw
Him heedless into a spangled shoal of dreams.
Therein, betimes, a spined and poisoned tail
In bubbling sweep may shard his skull, bestick
His heart, and send his headlong corse to ground
In midst the swirling nimbus of his blood.

   O Hosts on high, obtain for us stout bars
Of grace to make our souls all fast against
The mummery that yonder waits us. E'er
Before my sund'ring prow wave slow thy vans
In stately flight, my Guardian nigh; appall
Those thievish denizens below and look
Their miscreations back to Hell. Meseems
Thou urgest me to beg the ear of one
That lived, as I do yet, in flesh and time,
But one within the mountain's shadow of
Whose builded prodigies my deeds are as

The pebbled works and crimp thrown up of ants
Or eyeless moles. O sainted Thomas, child
Of Aquin, child of God, who now in sweet
Concent with angels descant far above
Th' eristic chirm of earth, incline those eyes
That nursed thy Herculean mind; observe,
Thou peer of the illuminating sun,
How parlous lies my road. I pray thee for
My speed ask fortitude of Him Who trod
Th' obedient sea and, swiftly quieting
The bully winds, drew Peter from the crowd
Of bumping waves. For that thy pow'rs informed
The flesh, thou wast of discourse straitly done
The emulated master. Who shall walk
The cobbles of thy narrow ways and walled
Will soon arrive the lucid square of truth.

　　Wherefore, what hour forth sea or sky shall burst
The dazzling image in my sight—when loom
Unseen shall breathe a doing in mine ear
And press the bellied sail—do thou, my Saint
In everlasting orison, request
For me such craft of discourse as may teach
Me whether of the warring origins
The inspiration comes. From this self steep,
Which thou and other few of giant race
Did build aloft, those after issue of
The Stagirite and thee scanned hard the surge
And made three aberrations whereinto
Unhappy poets stray. The first, for all
Perhaps the least in Heaven's disesteem,
Is but the reinless use of threading wild
Abnormities and casualties rare,

The sugared cates that feed the tooth for bare,
Disjoint adventure—for the wonder of
Occurrences and deeds to which no likes
On earth were ever seen. Oh, what is time
If not God's stay of that great whetted blade
Upthrown to lay the human crop at length?
Within this spacious gift, He cites all things
To season in the mellow month and soft.

    This fullness whither He will ev'ry of
His creatures ripen, each in sev'ral kind
And unto sev'ral measure, is, in sooth,
The imitation of His glories. Now
Th' unfurlèd host of nature, oft of freak
And foil put by their course, but hint our eyes
The copious land to which they make. And thus
The part of him that o'er this heaving waste
Would ply the nimble pen in numbers is
To show in act the mimic tendency
That God bestows upon His creatures all—
Indeed, t'exhort the imitation of
His Christ. For man no matter urges save
Redemption. Hence, when minstrel's matter is
The truths that nearly bear upon our souls,
'Tis storying the flesh was giv'n a will
Unbound, who therewith shapes a course for good
Or bad, that fitliest avails us men
To grasp the bias of the golden world
And fetch the long felicity in Heav'n.

    The poet true will take the sea at float
And tell an action like and self-sufficed—
In train of cause and inevasible
Effect—that, when his boat he shall have banked

Afar, he shall this part of Augustine
Have bodied out: For God has moulded us
To be His own, our hearts shall have no rest
Until they wear their lengthful way to Him
And in the arms of His sweet lenity
Repose them like the prodigal returned.

    O Thomas mine, near all whose thoughts would stand
Eternal law and full the famished clerk,
What wisdoms, what enlargements of the mind
Or soul has he that makes an idol of
The strange event and seldom? He will far
Extravagate through Faerie that from
The box he might e'er spring wry Jack. Along
An accidental roam of incidents,
He now perchance will have his hero to
A region lists and set him fierce at tilt
With headless knights, and now might give him o'er
To nerveless throes of passion for a may
Though he have neither seen nor spake her, but
Just spied her beauty's likeness brushed within
A locket's close. Though yielded it may be
That poets such will take the widow time
To wife and manly captain o'er the swells
To famous far the noble deed, as well
They might with keel but draw a circle on
The sea. For whiles they rove and touch upon
The many coasts of rare adventure, they
Forget or set at nought the poet's straight
And sacred purpose to the Mount Whose side
E'er pulses nectar to the parching tongue.

    Their talent dissipate in fleeting thrills,

They end at best by coyly harbouring
Where first they spread the spanking sail—no more
Percipient now than when they loosed for sea.
At worst, they end like rash Ulysses, who
Renounced the glowing hearthstone and with all
His ancient crew once more at bench and helm
Struck o'er the great, blind deep to find where he
Might graze the withered fruit that 'neath the Tree
Of Knowledge strow the dank, inhabited mould.
Upon a day, as they were sailing off
The wind a thousand leagues from charted tides,
A Mountain loomed upon their hungry stare;
And as they tilted nearer, frisking on
The little seas, there breathed a tempest forth
The slopes ahead that shortly span thrice round
The groaning ship, which by a whirlpit's maw
Was headlong gulfed, all hands aboard, their great
Incentor wild and clinging to a sheet.

 O thou that hammeredst iron proof against
The rams and bolts of error, fend us from
The second deviation witnessed by
Thy latter seed, who never stood this watch
But harmless and availed. Than errantries
Of knight fantastic—or he deftly play
The crimsoned axe or sweep the blushing lute—
This second wand'ring proves more arrant still,
Again more grave. The poet, weary of
The billowing way of action, will misprize
The grizel time; and, though he would not put
Her quite away, full oft he takes his leave
To seek the wanton moment's sooted eyes,
Her lips made shrill with paint. To passion he

Abandons him, as with his sorcerous tongue
He casts a glamour of infinity
About sensation; and, to spell away
The mind from very actualities,
He raises reveries unansw'rable
To reas'n or Heav'n's high Will. Thus robed around
With termlessness, the warrantable joys
Of recreation are upheaved upon
Inebrious shoulders and like strutting skins
Of wine are borne in lurching triumph to
A pantheon of follies, where upon
A pedestal they squat the idols of
An age. (Oh, vile and terrible to sight
Unsotted!) And, abjuring gen'ral truth,
The bard that would but feel must worship the
Particular—ere long, the fey: such things
As strange and fatal gleam. No longer does
He joy in fabling the sublimity
Of one inspirited in many; nay,
He only loves to verse the sev'ralty
Of things, nor will he deign to own therein
The unity, how large so'er it loom
Throughout. Ere long, he gratulates himself
As one so keenly passible as scarce
To be assorted with the kind of man.
The more abnormous the emotions of
This sagging jack-afloat, the quicklier
From battled poop he flourishes them to
The soapless multitude of normal breed
He scorns but unto whom will posture ay.
Sweet sun and saint, whose fame will tell what years
Remain this world, no bard shapes true his course,

Though he should sail the farthest seas of earth,
But stays within the homely wick of men.
Pray speed, O Lord, the faithful poet's clean
And ever-flying timber unto Thee!

    But cast a princely sight once more, great Saint
At such a bard as mads for sentience.
In search of ecstasies he rides from isle
To shimmering isle, each one unwonted more
And further witched than that he rummaged last.
Not long his ship may gently heave and set
At anchor ere upon the ocean line
Must glimpse that fat avernal grandly hight
Satiety, who lepers all delight
And pirates all this poet's treasured hopes.
The victim, letting groans and walling round
His eyes, once more makes sail to gain from his
Tormenter and another Lotus-Land
Invent. So far he wanders from the course
He charted first that ev'ry normal thing
He glances, ev'ry the sublimest and
The least, stands fair to touch him piteously
Upon the raw. Thus ever deeper bores
The maggot in this poet's musèd brain.

    The colourable objects of his quest
Are diversly th' Almighty, brotherhood,
The transcendental she (this latter if
His tide of humours flood to womanwards),
And, last, the woodlands wild. Communion all
Without himself he wants; but God for him
Is only immanent—but dwells within
The fabric of His vast creation, as
He were Himself a creature. And the vast

This poet gazes pales no object, for
His dogged fancy crowds it full with all
His woolly reveries and wishes, all
Which batten ruthlessly and graze it clean.
The universe is victuals to a sheep.
In fine, he is himself his universe;
His god is but himself. What need of grace?
Himself of kind is gracèd. Is not his heart
With sentiment awash? If haply reas'n
Or will he want, in russet liv'ry of
His dreams obsequious they wait. Now in
His soft Arcadian strain, he ofttimes sings
The brotherhood of Man, a creature of
His civic mood, a phasm quaintly like
Himself, impatient of such remoras
As venerable use and weariful
Moralities that dare to urge upon
A throbbing exquisite the carlishness
Of self-denial. Who, dear Saint, will not
Upon the stony way drag up and bear
The splint'ry burthen of his cross not long
Will keep his yielding heart from growing stark
As stone and last will hardly deign to draw
The merest sliver out his neighbour's quick.
And though this Perigot shall set his flock
A-bleat upon the passing gladness of
Fraternity and through his oat shall flute
Hortations to the world how they must to
Their feeling breasts their reeds accord and straight
An universal diapason breathe
Of brother's love, there follows straight in sad
Reality such scrannel din as should

All eared creation vex and harrow. Nought
There is so private and respective as
The heart, withal so vagrant. Wherefore how,
Thou burning phare, shall scattered be enleagued,
Or how conventional eccentric? Thence
Recoiling each from other in a harsh
Disownment, some through wild of Arcady
Will maze in several and gather wool
From wiry bramble, where their frighted dreams
And silly now seek refuge. Other some
That in the name of fair fraternity
Struck off their fathers' heads and rolled them 'neath
A trampling multitude of cattle fall
At strife among themselves—pull Phrygian caps
In mutual suspicion—till at length
A wily Hobbinol and mighty shall
Outtop his black-browed fellows and require
How they his brothers now must be or paint
Their crimson life upon his new-beat sword,
On which his governance to serve they smart
Bestow a kiss, in all fraternity.

    Near all such poets of this scatt'ring as
To dalliance propend conceit, each one,
A vap'rous nymph that leads his cap'ring heart
A pretty dance. In blue beyond his reach,
She glints the void intaglio of his dreams,
Whereof on earth no waxen woman can
He find t'accept the fair impression. Yet
Her planetary eyes keep ever quick
The livid flame within his breast. Between
Two deeps of blue the poet steers: above
His sail still smiles the high serene; beneath

The plowing strakes the hungry gulf still yawns.
O Patron blissfully at praise within
The bastion of God, who ne'er so nice
The plumb and level of thy reason pliedst
As when with Blood of the Incarnate Word
Thou here becam'st inebriate, pray, an
Th' All Knowing it shall like, incline and by
A still locution ask the poet spelled
Of wafting nymph if he can say from which
Cerulean burn the lucent eyes he stares.
His slippery heart has stroked and lullabied
His poppied wits to sleep, and now he weens
That upward bend his thirsting orbs to catch
The streams of Heaven's slaking influence.
In sorry sooth, he o'er the gunwale bends
His length to gaze the eyes that beckon 'neath
Th' abysm's lifting verge until with feet
In air he librates o'er perdition like
A giddy child. Whilst thus he drifts, he far
Outshears his elder precedent, who will
Indeed conceive a mistress for his knight,
But thrones her as a stainless damozel
Within a star-enwreathèd tow'r that by
Celestial filaments enlaced she might,
If blithely, heave her plated gallant as
A beetling lobster off the carnal ground
Of life. And so was trothless sense bound o'er
As handmaid unto spirit's airy sway.

 But spirit, all adust, is now haled down
In chains and chatteled 'neath the mired heel
Of sense grown insolent. As often as
This later bard shall gather to his breast

A rosy may that sweetly minds him of
His smiling dream, he sings her as the glass
Of translunary good, the mirror of
His feeling soul. He trills her thus till her
Inevitable kidney or her own
Chimera intervenes for thorns to show
Her weary and unworthy of his heed.

 O browsick he! betrayed to mis'ry by
His spectral fair, who softly laughs and fleets
Away, nor long omits to beckon. Or
In cold adieu he lip the hectic cheek
Of love despised, or in a fiery pique
His blistered front from scorn redeem, he casts
Away, as 'twere perforce, that he might find
His dream aflash within the dimpling pools
Of still another earthly maiden's eyes.

 And so, twice, thrice, and more he shall relive
This Cupid's tale until his wasting hopes
Once cordial shall languish throughly pricked
And bled, as pig-like he will needs swill down
The brimming stoup of flat futility.
And ne'er the She whose love he fondly hopes
Was in the smallest wise what bonny one
Of frame and soul drew living breath before
Him. Nay, and who than thou more swiftly sees
Consociate of angels, that the She
This poet weeps and sings will prove upon
A closer eye to be in very deed
His greedy self, all farded, veiled, and coy.

 At pains to ward the darts of ridicule
An histrionic pose he strikes amidst
The palace fall'n about his crimson ears.

And though the heart of whom he loved, and leaves,
Shall be opprest with shame or love unpaid,
Yet hardly can the humble thought engage
His mind to do for her avail, ne e'en
Put up for her a moment's pray'r: but he
Must wrap him in the weeds of woe; have done
With faithless humankind; and, bidding all
A frigid valediction, stalk away
To join those kithless and unfathered souls
That cloistered them within the hollow wild
The phantom wool to pluck. For now he would
Commune with that wherein it pleases them
To box the vasty name of Nature, e'vn
The stolid hosts of hills and trees, which prove
Betimes but cold to men and rooted fast
In unrelenting fealty to God.

    By sophistries and crooling song, he sends
The pickets of his heart and soul to sleep;
And though sometime he goes at large as on
His nimble four to bell his passions like
A fervid brute, he oftener reclines
To vegetate in golden reveries
With bushes. Thus, he holds himself for wise.
Not maidens now, who want a pliancy
Of will and intellect, but cataracts
Allure and thistledown compels, which will
Become as hinds to be in spirit rent
And eaten by a pride of metaphors.
What need to say to thee, thou sovran mind
In God secure, that not with boscage or
The writhen rock does this forlorn commune:
He does but congress with his tangled moods,

Admire as in a glass the crumbling chalk
That idly postures for a monument.
    As go the lives of men, no matter or
These votaries of feeling shall declare
For God or man or nymph or nature, they
Near ev'ry quivering sentient will in time
And all upon a sudden fetch aground
Before a restive barren of regret.
Sensation is the transcendental goal,
So strangely, so vertiginously felt
That eye should hear the setting sun, as if
The little conchs of mortal listening
Might catch Hyperion jolting to the verge
On rumbling wheels; that through the hours of ev'n
No poet's nose that shall inspire above
An open phial of attar but should look
The reeling song of ruddy-petalled flow'rs
Or keenly feel the booming humble-bee
About his furious and civic task;
That ear, engulfed alike, should weirdly eye
Sweet Progne's twittered arabesques and eft
Upon the breathless night the storied web
Of Philomela's mystic jargoning;
That tongue should smack the Muse's twang of wire
Or taste the feeble shriek of dainties milled
Between the clashing regiments of teeth.
(Thus, fain is ev'ry vatic bard of sense
Transcendent to be rid of storied deeds—
Of ev'ry whiff and peep of agency
That might his scarebabe, fell Ponderiact,
Arouse, who blames him for a craven and
A Sybarite whose duties all disowned

Are scarce the less to do.) But though a bard
Upon the main shall peer both long and prone
For raptures, he will ween in rue how full
As long as he shall run right stoutly buoyed
This side the veil of dissolution he
May never hope to word or e'en perchance
Be sensible of these obscure delights
Stirred to and mingled as with witch's wand,
All which thereat he hazards to account
Among the everlasting guerdons of
A blest eternity, as if the Lord
In mockery stood ready to bestow
Upon th' Elect the stone, the scorpion, of
A vulgar riot for their portion. Thou
Whose dow'r of mind was dawn to sunless souls
And whose much sanctity was noon, this gull
Assevers that his goal is Heaven high,
But surely 'tis himself. He longs, in truth,
T'include him fast within the closet of
His innest gaudy dreams and, like a tame
And bloodless cageling, nightly warble e'en
The substance of his minglements and moods
To ears beyond the veil that billows forth
His casement dark. To spell one's fellow men
This wise, howe'er, there needs a gramarye
The like whereof this bard has ne'er so much
As thought; and thus, although he would maroon
His sweating oar, slave discourse still misprized,
He needs must flog him into pulling through
An explanation lucid and direct
Of all those turbid synaesthetic joys
To be beyond this weary burgher's tale

Of earthly tedium. 'Twere better far
To put a nobler charge upon abused
Discursion, who besteads his master best
When he is bid to sweep the staring prow
Dead through a plotted trial of worthies, whose
Inweaving intercourse twixt swaddling bands
And winding sheet tries good from ill and soon
Describes in high-wrought web and many-hued
The very front of universal Truth,
Whose gaze serene gives men to quiet mind.
    Grown faint with duteously laying on
The bloody lash, which only feebles whom
It urges on, the jaded bard has waxed
Impatient of eternity and to
The whisp'ring strand near which he lately came
Aground he lends a languid eye; for might
Not here, he thinks, be haply found a means
The masterly avail of which should from
The irksome, explicative round of pull
And glide abstract his spleeny self, so keen
To roll in boundless multitude? But more
By much, he aches to verse in ev'ry of
His kindred ears as veninous a brew
Of moods inebriant as ever sod
Within an iron heart. A pregnant while
He poises what to do; and then, with hope
That he should light at last upon his legs,
From off his timber's edge he leaps and lights
Upon the sand. Scarce inland has he trod
Beyond the sea-beat yards when straight there strikes
His dazzling eyes a radiant form come nigh.
It is the Lady Circe, and the isle

His tousled bark has lurched upon is just
That Aea, seat of all her doings fey,
Whence bards set forth upon the desperate third
Of those three errancies thine issue named.
    With blandishments and graceful becks, she has
Him to her tower. Stupidly, he goes
Much like those sacrificial bulls of yore
Ringed, wreathed, and ponderously biddable
To blood-washed altars builded to appease
The gods of Hell. Now Circe, comliest
Of timeless hags and ancient minion of
The angels damned, by witchwork would become
This poet's evil muse. Right soon he tells
His tedium and sighs his dearest wish,
The twain to her well-known or e'er he spake.
In soothful flow of words, she prays him to
Repose his misery in her and speaks
That he shall have his heart's long hope within
That glooming, bluer deep that hissed before
His sev'ring prow but gaily flashes in
Presentiment upon his mudded keel.
    Now warming to her work, she plies him thus:
Such sophic heads as he know how that vast
Of blue aloft, suffused and flooded with
The ever-streaming brilliance of the sun,
Could hardly be the haunt to which he shows
Him naturally fain. Indeed, t'embrace
The wild'ring, dizzy joys he craves, he need
Not wait the fearful-singing blade that strews
The bent and bearded harvest flat. This side
The waxen shroud, his goal is hard at hand
In Ocean's deep and murk delights of mood

And synaesthetic gurging. See, thou Saint,
Who wardest well thy suppliants' reasonings
Till Heaven's orbs and crosses round their minds,
How now this flatt'ring coz'ner twines him with
Her sophistry, which draws and cumbers like
That boneless fish whose suckered arms grow forth
A soft and bagging head. In fine, she vows
That peace eludes him that he yet retains
His weariful drudge, discursion and, great shame
To say, indites as he were dragged e'en now
At imitation's florid wheel, which bears
The brazen car of tyranny and runs
The lyric fair of self-evincement o'er,
The stoic world whereat by grief at last
Undone at loss of this Melpomene's
So intimate, withal so instantly
And widely warbled lay. But he turn out
His oar and greasy turnspit, quite refuse
To mount the wearing tumult of the sea,
And sink beneath the billows blue, he ne'er
Shall have his happiness, which sole within
The sweet enfoldments of that deep-laid port
Of joy may be possessed. More nimble than
Arachne bold, she weaves her tissue of
Vermillion philosophic lies dropt o'er
With golden flatteries, a standard brave
Yet one beneath the streaming insolence
Of which the breathless poet somewhat fears
T'enlist his easy shame. Perceiving then
The ague of a moment's fear hunt out
His newly covert heart, she makes a smile
Behind which she convenes her inward pow'rs.

She bears to be his only friend, to word
Her simple heart, and this all only for
His good. Would he, a cavalier of fame,
Decline to put his fellow suitors to
The blush? And like the fabled fox, would he
Then slink inglorious away the while
Protesting that the scented bays by muse
Enwreathed to grace the Orphic brow are but
A sere and cankered mat of weeds? Not long
May souls as finely sensible as he
Ignore desires they know cannot be reined.
He would demean him ill in trepidly
Abridging him of aught that goes to make
Him throughly self-apaid. Thus, whenso he
Shall hear the far sirenic notes at play
Upon the lightsome gales, Oh, let him fend
The hands of his too-ready servant reas'n,
That meddling oar, who would his master's ears
Estop and straitly lash him to the mast!
The deeps of self the poet must descend;
But ere he shall implunge with silver shoals
To antic, he shall have of her a wand
Of wizard pow'r wherewith in poesy
To bear a god's dominion over all.

    So on she earwigs deeper still a hatch
Of further lies to lay that they might reel
The balance of his wheedled mind till it
Should lowly stoop to her. With warmth she vows
How first his sigil grandly sweeping, he
Will equal man and worm and star and weed.
In fancy thus declaring all the world
To be a fluid heap of sand, a dust

Of atoms 'neath his spirit's awful tread,
He will his senses' five great bartizans
Embattle, whence like Rhenish brigands he
Might spoil at will the passing argosy
Of treasures to his purpose. Draining forth
The upward orb of boist'rous doing, they
Will through the narrows to the downward orb
Of lang'rous musing droop. Thence farther will
They plummet, through the lowest nethers of
His soul, until the very ground of his
Unreason they shall heap, where swim just off
The phosphorous slime the shapes of nameless dreams.
   'Tis of his poet's mystery, she lips,
To give these swimming dreams, say rather moods,
A tenancy within these looted pearls,
Which thus possessed and by their tenants warped
Fair out of countenance are then become
The very stuff of poesy, what things
May emblem and imply to fellow hearts
Those synaesthetic states that chastely bloom
As long as he shall make his soul's stout door
Full fast against the shameless bravery
Of time. And she will lift the burthen of
Composing from his bended shoulders, where
Rough reason plumped it down as if upon
A blinkered beast before he urged him o'er
The waste with thumpings of his iron rod.
    For now no more is here to do than from
The drunken pen quite hazardously to
Asperse the vacant page with mystic glyphs,
To make a heavenscape of revery
That may bedew the parching world beneath

With fatal influence. Mispainting thus
With oily versatility, she worms
Yet farther 'cross the front of truth to tell
Him how in numbers thus appearing he
Shall be to angels liked, e'vn that great host
In fires of refusal still aswim,
A battle casqued and sharply horrid yet—
But delicately pensive therewithal—
Who scorned to look the blinding Tyranny
That thrones Him in the apse of Heav'n and hence
Betray themselves so proudly gripple of
Their inward galaxies of forms innate,
The glinting coins of intellection true
And instant, all without the plane of time.
And if his noble moods shall want somewhen
An intuition's iron consonance
With fact, the sheer intensity of his
Poetic constellations shall upheave
A fierce, titanic bore that shall upon
Its monstrous shoulders bear him hurtless through
The grinding narrows of ungenerous
Reality. (Oh, most egregious lie!)
    For that he came within this world a gross
Extrusion from the void and void within
Of those ideas wherewithal the sheer
Created spirits had been found, he must,
'Tis roundly claimed, to prove the worth of that
His fancy may invent take counsel with
His reason. Here her orbits look as set
With living coals, such eyes as beaming from
The Aegis might have stared the world to stone.
She shrills how reason is a grimy shroff

That twixt his teeth delights a dream new struck
To bend and show it for an obolus
Would hardly have a blackguard's soul across
The livid flow of Styx. No right has reas'n,
She vows, to hobble Pegasus though sprung
From monstrous blood, for throbbing art may not
Be stilled. Thus, breathing feeble arguments
As they were fire, she tells her bard right out
That he must never reck the morrow, no
Nor grave monition said alow within
His heart. Before aught else he must not hold
Him unto aught responsible. He must
Reject all things would impudently put
A fealty upon him. 'Tis but he,
She hoos, must be the monarch of his soul.

    And now, dear Guide, she fancies that she hears
Just off the summit of her vap'rous head
The rustling wings of Victory with bays
In hand her brow to bind. The poet now
Shows suasible to any urgency
She fain would speak. And thus, in clamant tones
That cite the pulsion of his blood, she bids
Him to his boat again, which gently rolls
Upon an evening tide becrimsoned of
The dying sun. He must embark, spread sail,
And run until beneath his keel shall gape
The ocean's boundless deep, o'er which arrived
He will at once forsake his ancient prore
And all the nuisance of her gnarlèd ropes
And ritual (what feeling soul could long
Remain her master?) and will slip for ay
And o beneath the darksome swells. This last

Of her malarias exhaled, he hastes
Away her urgent will to work as he
By barking terriers were chased. Ere long,
Above the gulf he rides the tossing deck
Once more, but rides forgetful of the boat
That bears him up, her hold of noble words
And numbers neat, and heedless how in long
Despite of naiads, spouts, and sea-drakes she
Once fastly bare him dry and homewards o'er
Old Ocean's hugely rolling sinews. Now
Uncordial to any gale would hie
Him on, he furls and in a wanton rite
Of malice breaks th' unfeigning sail stone with
His warping wand. At once he drops beshrewed
And like a boulder through the fluent veil
To dwell where dungeoned madness grins amidst
The shrouding legions of the dead and damned.

    O Thomas glad, thou beaming ruby blushed
Of God's sweet ravishing, ye angels blest,
Bright diamonds whose ev'ry face afire
At once retains and still to God returns
Its sev'ral beam of fervid blessedness
Come forth the furnace of His infinite
Completeness, prithee ask a grace of Him
Whom all we love (though I a sinner yet)
That might this poet gently mesh and rap
Clean out the ruthless, breathless sea of self.

    But thou, O region angel here beneath,
The guardian of this lost to view, as lost
To grace, meseems in prompt obedience to
Divine decree, thou frownest now; for lo,
The welkin beetles o'er with sudden cloud

That sables all the main. And sure thy breath
It is that yonder stirs the shivering waste.
O saints and hallowed quires on high, behold
A funnelled, fatal cloud in awful gyre
Descending as it were a finger of
Th' Omnipotent! Whilst rooted in the pall
That streams above, it lights in furious spin
Upon the dreadful sea and scours forth
Inscribing "Havoc" on the tortured waves.
From out this roaring tongue of wind, within
The course this airy stylus now describes,
Methinks I hear and read the sturdy kind
Of praise it soon will render up to God's
Omnipotence. It makes direct for that
O'erclouded rag of sand, proud Circe's haunt,
Erewhile deliriously shimmering i'
The flaming air. Its mistress high upon
Her stony keep, descries th' approaching harm.
Though inly stunned she gloriously makes
As if she had it in contempt. But now
Her liver quails within the gripe of fear,
And she recourses unto desp'rate plaints
And curses dire. Behold the storm with all
Its nameless terrors hard upon her. She
Would play the gorgeous heroine and clutch
A writhing aspic to her milken breast.
O fie upon pretense! With bloody nails
She flays her cheeks and howls her panic grief
At Heav'n, which herewith bears to this accurst
The deadly issue of her labours. Full
Upon the isle, the wrackful pillar moves;
Though late it gathered up the frantic swells,

It now uptears a whirl of biting rock
And sand, wherewith accoutred cap-a-pie
It coils the tower round in fierce embrace
And looses ev'ry mortared stone. In brief
Relentment, lo, it suffers all the pile
To drop unstrung upon the gasping earth!
Now even as the fabric nodded to
Its thund'rous fall, the whilom chastelaine
Was borne distract amongst the horrors of
The welter's upward drafts, wherein she makes
Such shrieks as sole the tempest's mightful throat
Can dumb. Immit, O Saint and angels, yet
Another prodigy: At ev'ry mouth
And angry grin wherewith she wries her face
Erst fair, she moulds without advertency
A new and hideous front that squarely charts
Her deep-laid villainies; the fleets of tears
She streams her rose-, nay blood-dyed cheeks withal
Engrave in jagged, ever-during wakes
The vagrant courses of her greedy gulls.
And wheresoe'er her victims unto death
Implunged appears a fiery pock. Above
The anger sedulously furrowing
Her brow, the locks entwine in motion wrought
Of more than urgent wind; for see, they change
By one and one to flickering vipers, which
Now one, now other drop the head to sting
The face of who without all bowels lured
Unhappy men to Hell. Now blown aslant
The boist'rous, terror-breathing night, she hurls
To seaward like a thunderstone and through
The surges bowls, O holy ones, as if

From cannon's maw she had been vomited
Ahead a blust'rous rout of writhing flame.

    The tutelary vicar of these skies
Serenely curbs his snorting meteors
Of fire and deluge and, relaxing all
The whirlblast's twisted sinew, hies away
The silent herd of cloud. Quite gone that old
And awless jade that ever lessened grace
In men and poesy and must with long,
Incogitable pangs once pay within
The cold for-ever of perdition. Now,
This vision flown, though scarce to be forgot,
Mine eyes the clear, discovered sky survey,
Vast floors of deepest dye besprent across
With living gems as from most princely Hand.
To me they show as symbols of yourselves;
As, shining o'er the waters strown and still,
They smile me out of fear and eager to
Be down and set upon the main to tell,
As well to live, the course of martyrdom
And glory far above the poet shrined
Within himself, a rigid corpse entombed.

    But look you! the approaching lord of day
Begins as with a seep of woad to hue
And clarify the eastern night; and though,
In turn, the many-schooling stars begin
Like dolphins blithe and debonair to sound
Within this tiding blue of morn, one Star
In undiminished oriency shines
Just o'er the golden nimbus of the dawn.
More pure, more bright she beams than ever shone
The brightest of those flames that yonder bow

And through the purpled arras take their leave.
Indeed, ye interceding gods, since that
Becrimsoned shut of yestere'en, no star,
Methinks, has shone till now. By grace of God,
This far yet hugely coruscating fire
Cites not my heart to wonderment, which oft
A gaping innocency will pretend
Whilst in the tickling, agitable soul
It plies the thistle curiosity
To evil purpose. Nay, within this breast
Her influential beams a holy awe
Inspire, the seed of sweet humility.
    Whatever mingled exhalations of
My waking nerves may rise, I would not set
Them running up the sky like spectral beasts
Of earth to ravish and possess a star,
Which thus become an emblem twisted of
My vanity must meanly hobble in
A clubfoot row of numbers. Rather am
I fain to like this morning lamp unto
That pure mosaic gaze that shows within
The golden air aglitter high above
The altars of Byzantium. Dear my Saint
And angels aerial, to me this fire
Of purity may fitly emblem One
That dwells an infinite remove from all
My lowness, One withal the Crucified
Ere forth He breathed His sacred soul to God
His Father, gave (oh, gift unhoped!) for mine
Own Mother mild. O Mary, burning heart
And pierced, who beaconest the toiling prows
That crawl the surly seas across the port

Of God to scry, O heart that shin'st above
The gladsome, circling quires that sing thee Queen
Of all creation, haste, I pray, thine ear
Of grace t'incline to me, confiding how
Though sure I kneel this morn thy meanest child
Thou'lt hear and help as ay. The lightening hour
Is come wherein, so grant thy Son, in calm
Expectance I shall pick my downward way
(Right heedfully lest the balm should spill that brimmed
This brittle phial my heart along my wake
Of pray'r). When next shall flood the cove beneath,
Which slumbers still and dreams, I ween, the gests
And hazards high of youth, I would upon
My timber's deck the hempen fingers of
The harbour's sleepy ward be casting off
And heaving forth a sail to meet the airs
Of aureate morn. O blessed Cynosure!
The Guide at once and Inspiration of
Thy poets' hearts, when yet a little I
Shall loose for sea 'twill be thy radiance bids
Me forth to meet my God across this gulf
And sweeping flood of dreams and deeds. O see
Above the earth's red rim he hugely springs,
The symbol of thy Son, the Christ of God,
And closes ev'ry eastward-gazing eye
With instant awe this Easter of the day!
My hand as e'er in thine, sweet Mother of
My bursting heart, I prithee lead me down
And gently to my going hence to reach
The harbour of my Saviour's opened Side.
    And thorough all my careful days upon
The wayward blue pray send me towardly gales

Of inspiration and the grace to keep
A poet's present hand upon the wheel,
To keep the symmetry and rhythm of
A course that may in numbers body forth
To men the glorious tragedy of one
That dies to self as highest Love brings down
The peen of grace upon the metal of
His firèd soul with love and martyrdom
Candescent. Whilst I sail the heaving waste—
That blear and fishful sea—pray scatter all
The shining tribes that promise hurt. Thou know'st
One side my way will loom grey Scylla, she
The bard o'ernice mishallows for the One,
The rock of gen'ral truth—for men, how all
Their happiness is found imbosomed in
The sweet convention of their wills with God's
Illuminous Mind. Upon a doleful day
Great ages since, that Circe that a trice
Ago was helped to fetch a timely leap
To seawards of the tempest's roar was spurned
By Glaucus, who to Scylla was more true
Than sailstone to the Pole, for which despite
Not Glaucus but th' unhappy Scylla bare
The witch's greenest hate. Fell Circe weaved
An evil word and stirred it full within
The waves in which fair Scylla oft beguiled
The scorching hours of afternoon. Ere long,
Then, Scylla bathed as she was wont and whilst
Disporting found her sprouting forth a zone
Of monstrous heads. Thus hideously spoiled
She rose in single, monumental dread
And loathing, whereupon she turned into

A cape of stone, from thence to stand a tomb
Of fear and port for ev'ry pavid bard
Whose blood within him clings do he but ween
Unwonted stir beneath the tireless pomp
Of ocean. Thus above the waters she
Has lowered ever eft, say, rather, o'er
The toils; and oft she muses how they quite
Enough had done had they no more than buoyed
And cooled her sweltered limbs—when yet a limb
She owned. These flowing toils, to usher on
My argument, dear Mother, are a strait
In which hard by the bank opposing whirls
Charybdis, cleped as well the Many, eye
Of Ocean, where the treble errancies
Abide whereof I late bespoke and long
Th' angelic Thomas. Round this reeling pit
They madly foot a tarantelle to which
They bid all poets passing nigh, the wise
Of whom this invitation spurn and with
An equipoise of mind their course to God
Maintain. Alas, that coward crew forespoke,
Poor pidgeonhearts, oft stand too much in fear
Of coming nigh Charybdis. Like a fox
In eggs, dismay their mettle mouths in shards
And takes the worthy lap of their resolve.

 It longs to him would come most near the sun
To call such gentles forth the fiery air
As in a stately dance of doings may
Display the One of universal truth
Become embodied in the Many. Hence,
No course is his but that he pained his mind
To chart before he stood away from port

To track his foaming way the vast of blue
Across, nor boldly bearing off from his
Career to foot it with the treble fiends
Beneath—in impious despisal of
The One, nor canting off in terror that
The Many morrice all too nigh, but, like
An arrow, sailing all between and thus
Inerrably to Christ, the archetype
Of ev'ry worthy tale, or sad or blithe.
 Upon such day as offers high revolt
Against a generation's weary use
Of welt'ring with the nereids three within
The watery gyre, it tides not rarely that
A bard by fashion mewed but puts away
For Scylla's frowning heights, which, when he fetch,
A vengeance falls him sore as swift. While yet
He closes with her granite flank, behold!
From forth an antre sighing pestilence
A grisly drake its stone-eyed head protends
And grinning beastlywise invades the boat.
With holders flashing in its reeking jaws,
It rapes him from the deck and casts him down
At length upon the iron strand. In voice
That bleeds his ears the monster booms how he
Must ever cast his troubles on its care,
How, whenso he shall ply the glinting flood,
He must great Scylla coast, nor never draw
Aught nearer to Charybdis, coiling and
Voracious, than the flowing purlieus hard
Along the base of Scylla's frozen stare.
At once the poet vows away his will
And gladly hears as from an oracle

How he must put that mistress of deceit,
Proud-mind imagination, to the ban;
For she, oh make no doubt, was ever leagued
With those three limbs of Satan swimming yond
Within the wreathing waters, where they quire
To ev'ry bard that passes nigh their fair
Mendacities, their amiable lies.

    In accents that announce the pedant, the
Appalling worm assevers how there sole
Requires a method wherewithal the bard
May sing the universal all without
Imagination's rage and fury. Here
The slavering beast, which joyed of yore to foul
Bright Scylla's bloom, a dusty treatise puts
Upon the bard, within the crowding leaves
Whereof are charactered in close array
A regiment of rules, the myrmidons
Of regularity. He hears that when
He shall have schooled him in these canons, he
Shall verse and stave build high by hurtling dint
Of cold mechanic skill, without so much
A puff of troublous inspiration as
Should stir the down of eaglet's wing. If I
May instance thee a rule that in the eye
By Scylla awed looms far more terrible,
O cause of all our joy, than any else,
One dare not ripened nature imitate
Direct. The poet must recourse instead
To paradigms, to wit, those bards of eld
That burst upon the buoyant wing and scaled
The heights of morn till, planing on the breath
Of angels through the vasts above, they looked

Upon the noontide blaze of heaven. Now
No doubt can be how th' imitation of
Such spirits by the fledgling bard both meet
And furthersome has been so it have made
Him love the truth and have so far from damped
His inward fires of high conceit as it
Should fan them brighter still. Thou knowest well,
Who tak'st the humbled bard to mercy, that
This narrow-heart of scales and coils will wreak
This rule upon its staring toy that he
Should still keep cold his forge and dark. For should
He set himself to glass direct the full
Accomplishment that nature purposes,
Though ever only hints to mortal heads,
He needs must court the fructifying airs
Of inspiration. Such audacity
His bilious lord will never stomach, for
Its bloodless charge might feel the spoom of mad
Charybdis and disturb his hearers with
A word or do unguessed. The poet quelled
Must coolly fall a-copying the books
Of all his betters. He must prise the lids
Of coffers not his own and thence abstract
A diction and fair poetries of myth
That, if his mind shall nothing forgetive
Or aught deep-going be, that is, shall be
A faithful liege to Scylla, he will but
Employ for pretty ornaments to trick
The tedium of his muse-forsaken verse.
    O thou that trod and crushed th' insinuant brow
Of writhing Hell, what lies has Satan left
Unhissed within the ears of men? This drake,

An image of his own tyrannic self,
Is certes e'en that blood-eyed fee-faw-fum,
A conscience miscreate, which he will put
As hard on wretches kindly finikin
As on such bards as dread all multitude
And motion of the sea. 'Tis true as sad
How flush imagination given o'er
To its devices to Charybdis will
Recourse and riot with the fuddlecaps
That reel therein. But by one beaming drop
Of the illimitable deep of grace
That flooded forth thy Son's most holy Wounds,
Imagination shall be throughly cleansed
And, riding sure upon the shoulder of
That orbèd tide, be to the middest clime
Conveyed of Ocean's race twixt rock and gurge,
Upon which midsea reason's timber shall
Abide so it shall be, in happy turn,
Pressed gently thither fore a mist of grace
By thee aspersed. Imagination to
The midst attaining, reas'n shall bring her straight
To wife and, following the roister of
The merry dolphins, to the leavy Side
That hangs above the orient reaches of
The wave. Their issue will be poems of
A man, to time, the scroll 'neath reason's quill,
Both wived and true, nor feigning timeless pow'r
Of seizing fast a fiery sooth as swift
As e'er an angel writes a levin bolt
Across the sky, no tale or discourse gone
Before. To none but spirits pure belongs
This pow'r of intuition, strung with all

Its airy, easy sinew. As all minds
By Heaven had to wisdom understand,
The intuitions that the bard of sense
O'erfined makes arrogant to call a grasp
Of truth, as they were e'en the noonlight of
Angelic intellection, are but blind
Sensation tasted o' the sudden and
In thorough want of concord with the real.

O fairest Flow'r of Heaven's hue, O real
And never feigning, whom I whisper beads
Of love and obsecration rathe and late,
Herewith I drop swift steps to strand and sea.
An humble birth, to Him I follow thee.

MASTER NICHOLAS
CONTRA MUNDUM

Since Christendom with pocks of heresy
O'erspread—th' infernal Maggot batt'ning on
Its heart—hath fall'n at heavy length to dree
A scourge of cank'rous chastisement, how, John,
Shall thy begotten Nicholas abide,
Who once must quit thy gates to crawl below
That gnostic eye and old upreared in pride
And quick with ill as th' living gleeds that strow
The marl of Hell? Tho' thou and Anne above
Your darling wake more fierce than e'er that dam
That suckled infant Rome, how may your love
Ensteel him? Lo, I need but word this sham
Of thought to hear its hollow faith; Who thwarts
Th' red Worm can headlong pride as it were orts.